The
Little Way
of
SAINT THÉRÈSE
of
LISIEUX

Readings for
Prayer and Meditation

Compiled and Introduced
by John Nelson

Liguori
LIGUORI, MISSOURI

Published by Liguori Publications
Liguori, Missouri
www.liguori.org

First published in Great Britain under the title *The Arms of Love With
St. Thérèse of Lisieux,* copyright 1997 by Darton, Longman & Todd Ltd,
1 Spencer Court, 140–142 Wandsworth High Street, London SW18 4JJ.

Library of Congress Cataloging-in-Publication Data

Arms of love with St. Thérèsa of Lisieux.
  The little way of Saint Thérèsa of Lisieux : readings for prayer and
meditation / compiled by John Nelson
      p.   cm.
  Originally published: The arms of love with St. Thérèsa of Lisieux.
London : Darton, Longman & Todd, 1997.
  Includes bibliographical references.
  ISBN 978-0-7648-0199-0
  1. Meditations. 2. Spiritual life—Catholic Church. I. Nelson, John,
1931– . II. Title.
BX2182.2.A76 1998
248.3—dc21   97–32384

Printed in the United States of America
17 16 15 14 13 / 14 13 12 11 10

All royalties from sales of this book go to the copyright holder The Little
Way Association, London, for the purpose of its support and care of
missionaries.

Liguori Publications, a nonprofit corporation, is an apostolate of
the Redemptorists. To learn more about the Redemptorists, visit Redemp-
torists.com.

Love is the origin and source of all good things.
Whoever walks in love can neither stray nor be afraid.
Love guides, love protects, love leads to the end.

from the Office of Readings, Feast of St. Stephen

Your arms, my Jesus, are the elevator
which will take me up to Heaven.
There is no need for me to grow up; on the contrary,
I must stay little, and become more and more so.

St. Thérèse of Lisieux

Contents

Acknowledgments ix

Introduction xi

What Is the Little Way? 1
Within the Reach of All 3

1. Joyful Humility As a Little Child of God 5

Introduction 7
Remain a Little Child Before Our Father 8
Take Refuge As a Little Child 10
To Be His, One Must Be Small 12
Love Shines Out Through Little Souls 14
A Little, Short, New Way to Heaven 16
In Utter Littleness, Gaze Upon Love 18
Love Chooses a Multitude of Little Souls 19
A Small Grain of Sand, an Atom 21
Lose Your Little Nothingness in His All 23
Be Poor, With Nowhere to Lay Your Head 25
God Upholds Little Souls 27
A Little Lamp Can Cause a Fire 28

Contents

Realizing My Nothingness More 30
God Shows Me My Weakness 32

2. Bold Confidence in God's Mercy and Loving Kindness 35

Introduction 37
I Know What to Believe About His Mercy and Love 38
God Is Even Kinder Than You Think 40
Be Simple With the Good God 41
Love Alone Can Make Us Pleasing to God 43
Always Have Confidence in God 44
What Have I to Fear Then? 46
The Way Is All of Trust and Love 48
It Is Good to Feel Weak 50
Compassion for Our Wretchedness 51
A Wind of Love, Faster Than Lightning 53
Jesus Must Be Our Reward 55
The Smallest Thing Is Precious to Him 57
Do Not Be Afraid of Rising Too High 58
Full Sail on the Sea of Confident Love 60

3. Tranquil Trust in the Actions of God's Limitless Love 63

Introduction 65
Only Trust Will Bring Love 66
All One Has to Do Is Love 68
The Heart Is Opened by Love Alone 70

Contents

At the Heart of the Church Is Love 72
He Loves Us Even to Folly 73
Love Pushed Even to Heroism 75
The Proof of Love 77
Love, Even to Folly 79
Your Heart Is Made to Love Jesus 80
Our God, Our Heart's Guest 82
Tell Him That You Love Him 84
Love Him More Than Self 85
Love Lives in Us 86

**4. Persistence in Prayer As a Simple Raising
   of the Heart to God 89**

Introduction 91
Prayer Unites the Soul With God 93
Meditate on the Gospel 94
Prayer Uplifts the World 96
A Simple Prayer for Others 98
Love Draws Us to Pray for Others 99
Prayer Works Miracles 101
Only God Supplies All Needs 103
Jesus Supplies, Moment to Moment 105
Throw Straws on the Fire of Love 107
Jesus' Peace Never Leaves 108
Merely a Sigh, a Prayer of the Heart 110
Offer Everything, in Happy Praise 112

Contents

5. Daily Practice of the Little Way of Love 115

Introduction 117
Love Must Act 118
The Truly Poor Are Happy 119
God Loves Others Through Us 121
Giving Love for Jesus 123
Do Everything to Give Pleasure to Jesus 125
Unselfish Love Is Joyful 126
Love Others As Jesus Loves Them 127
Love and Do Not Judge 129
Offer the Merits of Others to Jesus 131
A Strange Courage 133
Serving Jesus in Others 135
Love in Adversity 137
Washed by Love 139

Sources and Bibliography 141

Acknowledgments

The quotation on the title page from a sermon of St. Fulgentius of Ruspe is taken from the text in the Office of Readings of the Divine Office for the Feast of Saint Stephen, and is used by kind permission of the Catholic Hierarchies of England, Wales, Ireland, and Australia.

The extracts from Scripture are taken from the *New Jerusalem Bible*, published and copyright 1985 by Darton, Longman & Todd Ltd., London, and Doubleday & Co. Inc., and are used by kind permission of the publishers.

The extracts from *The Story of a Soul,* translated by Michael Day, Cong. Orat., are used by kind permission of Anthony Clarke Publishers, Wheathampstead, England.

The extracts from *St. Thérèse of Lisieux, Her Last Conversations,* translated by John Clarke, O.C.D., copyright 1977 by Washington Province of Discalced Carmelites, Inc., are used by kind permission of the publishers ICS Publications, 2131 Lincoln Road, N.E., Washington D.C. 20002, U.S.A.

The extracts from the *Collected Letters of Saint Thérèse of Lisieux,* translated by F. J. Sheed, are used by kind permission of Sheed and Ward Ltd., Publishers, London, England.

The extracts from *The Imitation of Christ* by Thomas à Kempis, translated by Betty I. Knott, are used by kind permission of HarperCollins Publishers Ltd., London, England.

Introduction

For many, saints may seem not to be good news. Their lives, often marked by complex spirituality, austerities, and penances, may appear admirable but exaggerated and irrelevant to the practical pursuits of the majority of Christians and others who try to be good amid the hurly-burly of life in the world. The saints of visions, revelations, and miracles may seem to put the achievement of holiness beyond the capacity of the ordinary person in humdrum daily life.

But the pursuit of spiritual wholeness—holiness—was not always so complex. Early Christians realized the simplicity of the good news of Jesus Christ, and strove to unite themselves with Him, imitating Him and testifying 'to the resurrection of the Lord Jesus with great power' (Acts 4:33). So Saint John could exclaim, "see what great love the Father has lavished on us by letting us be called God's children—which is what we are!" (1 John 3:1), emphasizing that everyone whose life is upright is a child of God.

If Saint John is the apostle of love, Saint Thérèse of Lisieux is the saint of love. Do not be deflected by the somewhat sentimentalized icon of her created by earlier devotees. She was tough-minded, direct, devoid of pretence and pretentiousness, matured in practicality and honesty. She had a real sense of fun and humor, even relishing the ridiculous, and her company was cheerful; for had not Saint Teresa of Avila said, "God save us from gloomy saints!"

Her life and teaching focus on the roots of our faith in Jesus Christ, who came to call sinners; ate with them; taught them; and called them His little ones. Pope Pius X named Thérèse as the greatest saint of modern times, but in the eyes of her contemporaries she appeared to live an uneventful, ordinary life as a provincial nun. Nevertheless, within a few decades she became one of the most loved of the saints. It is only little more than a century since she discovered "a short, direct, new way" to perfection, a "little way" available to everyone in any state and walk of life. She affirmed that Jesus alone had given her this inspiration. In His earthly ministry He had urged us to become as little children. Thérèse understood that little children cannot perform great deeds, but can and do give great love. She had learned from Saint John of the Cross that "love is repaid by love alone." So she confidently pursued the little way of love of a child of God, saying that everything she did in this way must be possible for any ordinary person like herself.

Thérèse was a forerunner of the Second Vatican Council and the present renewal of the Church by the Holy Spirit, marked as it is by fresh emphasis upon the significance and impact of the Scriptures. The Scriptures fired Thérèse's spiritual ideas, and she gained inspiration and confirmation from them. She carried a copy of the Gospels over her heart. She wrote that her chief resources were the Scriptures and *The Imitation of Christ*. The latter was written in the early fifteenth century, the product of a widespread religious renewal among clergy and laity who sought a more vital and direct experience of God in a devotional spirit based on His personal care of, and call to, each individual.

To this day the *Imitation* is one of the most widely read of books and, like the Bible, belongs to the dynamic spiritual heritage of Christians of all traditions and outlooks.

Consequently this present volume comprises a selection of the saint's writings and sayings, setting them in the context of the Scriptures and *The Imitation of Christ*. Beginning with a brief description as an introduction in each case, it explores the Little Way, and its five core elements, "planted in love and built on love," as Saint Paul expressed it. This progressive journey through the Little Way, can be made as daily readings for encouragement, inspiration, and prayer.

The texts are provided with references to the source books (listed on page 141). It is hoped that the reader, if not already acquainted with our saint, will wish to explore further her life, her sayings and writings, and her inspirational resources. Therefore a list of further available books is also given.

Pope John Paul II has urged us to "recognize the presence of the Holy Spirit at work in the efforts of all those who try to live the Gospel in their own state of life." Saint Thérèse and the Little Way are gifts of the Holy Spirit to encourage us all to try to live the Good News in the simplicity and profundity of the Way followed by our earliest brothers and sisters during the dawning years of the Christian faith.

JOHN NELSON
AUGUST 1996

What Is the Little Way?

Just at this time, filled with joy by the Holy Spirit, he said:
"I bless you, Father, Lord of heaven and of earth,
for hiding these things from the learned and the clever
and revealing them to little children.
Blessed are the eyes that see what you see,
for I tell you that many prophets and kings wanted
to see what you see,
and never saw it;
to hear what you hear,
and never heard it."

Luke 10:21,23–24

Saint Thérèse said this about her Little Way:

I t is the way of childlike self-surrender, the way of a child who
sleeps, afraid of nothing, in its father's arms. "Whoever is a
little one, let him come unto me" (Proverbs 9:4), says the Holy
Spirit through the lips of Solomon, and the same Spirit of Love
tells us also that "to him that is little, mercy is granted" (Wisdom 6:7).

The Story of a Soul, XI, 151

In her writings and sayings, Saint Thérèse teaches "a little way
to heaven, very short and direct, an entirely new way," having
found "an elevator to take me straight up to Jesus, because I am
too little to climb the steep stairway of perfection…. Your arms,
my Jesus, are the means which will lift me up to heaven. There
is no need for me to grow up; on the contrary, I must stay little,
and become more and more so."

Introduction

The Little Way to spiritual health is that of a child of God who humbly welcomes its utter inability, weakness, and poverty as a little one. It is boldly confident in its total dependence on the goodness, limitless love, and action of its heavenly Father. Such a child of God desires only His Will, and to live solely through love and for love. Since love drives out fear, it never fears the justice of God, knowing that He comes to save His little ones.

The core elements of the Little Way are these:

1. Joyful humility as a little child of God;
2. Bold confidence in God's mercy and loving-kindness;
3. Tranquil trust in the actions of God's limitless love;
4. Persistence in prayer as a simple raising of the heart to God;
5. Daily practice of the little way of love.

> *A good deed done without love goes for nothing,*
> *but if anything is done for love,*
> *however small and inconsiderable it may be,*
> *every bit of it is counted.*
> *God considers what lies behind the deed,*
> *and not what is actually done.*
> The Imitation of Christ, Book 1, XV, 49

Introduction

Within the Reach of All

Well done, good and trustworthy servant;
you have shown you are trustworthy in small things;
I will trust you with greater;
come and join in your master's happiness.

Matthew 25:21

I shall no longer call you servants, because a servant does not
know the master's business; I call you friends, because I have
made known to you everything I have learnt from my Father.
You did not choose Me, no, I chose you;
and I commissioned you to go out and to bear fruit,
fruit that will last; so that the Father will give you anything
you ask Him in My name.

John 15:15–16

Saint Thérèse said the following about her Little Way:

I t's the way of spiritual childhood, it's the way of confidence
and total abandon. I want to teach to others the little means
that have so perfectly succeeded with me.

Said to Mother Agnes of Jesus, July 17, 1897

I feel that I am about to enter into my rest. But I feel especially
that my mission is about to begin, my mission of making God
loved as I love Him, of giving my little way to souls.

Said to Mother Agnes of Jesus, July 17, 1897;
the Saint died on September 30, 1897

I really feel now that what I've said and written is true about everything.

Said to Mother Agnes of Jesus, September 25, 1897

My way is sure and I was not misguided in following it.

*Said during her appearance to the Mother Prioress
of the Carmel of Gallipoli, January 16, 1910*

The voice of the Lord:
I will teach you the way of peace and true liberty.
The disciple: Do this, O Lord—I am eager to hear.
The Lord: Try to do another's will rather than your own.
Always choose to have less rather than more.
Always choose the lowest place and to be less than
    everyone else.
Always long and pray that the will of God
may be fully realized in your life.
You will find that the one who does all this
walks in the land of peace and quietness.
The disciple: Lord, you can do all things
and you always love to see the soul making progress—
increase the gift of grace, so that I can do what you say,
and work out my salvation.

The Imitation of Christ, Book 3, XXIII, 128

1

Joyful Humility As a Little Child of God

*It is not that we are so competent that we can claim
any credit for ourselves;
all our competence comes from God.*

I t is Jesus who does everything in me; I do
nothing except remain little and weak.

From a letter to Céline, July 6, 1893

*What joy and delight it is to serve God like this,
when it brings real holiness and freedom!*

The Imitation of Christ, Book 3, X, 111

Introduction

Thérèse based her Little Way on humility—not destructive self-denigration nor lack of self-confidence, but true humility. Humility puts us in our right condition, our proper place. That which is created, however great it seems, is infinitely less than its Creator and is dependent upon its Creator. That which is created gains all that it is only from the infinite plenitude of the Creator; it has nothing from itself. The created being is of itself weak, powerless, poverty-stricken and must discover its purpose and all it needs in the One who created it. "We must see ourselves as little souls which God must uphold from moment to moment." The more we accept our infinite littleness, the more we discover our unending, measureless value to Him who made us for Himself.

Thérèse taught that since God is Love, "it is proper to Divine Love to lower itself; hence the lower we are, the more we attract God." If we do not recognize our extreme littleness and if we attempt of our own selves to raise ourselves, we act against the Love which desires to lower itself fully to our supernatural littleness. "For this is how God loved the world: he gave his only Son" (John 3:16). "He must grow greater, I must grow less" (John 3:30), said John the Baptist when he announced the coming of Jesus.

As we come honestly to accept what we really are, we are able as children of God to share the complete joy which filled John the Baptist at the sound of the voice of the coming Savior. We can grow to love what we really are, as Thérèse delighted in being little, hidden, and unknown, even seemingly useless. In that way we most please our heavenly Father, who passionately desires to do all things for us who are unable to do anything of ourselves.

Remain a Little Child
Before Our Father

I shall not leave you orphans;
I shall come to you.
In a short time the world will no longer see me;
but you will see that I live
and you also will live.
On that day
you will know that I am in my Father
and you in me and I in you.
John 14:18–20

When asked to explain what she meant by "remaining a little child before God," Thérèse replied:

It is to recognize our nothingness, to expect everything from God as a little child expects everything from its father; it is to be disquieted about nothing, and not to be set on gaining our living. Even among the poor, they give the child what is necessary, but as soon as he grows up, his father no longer wants to feed him and says: "Work now, you can take care of yourself."

It was so as not to hear this that I never wanted to grow up, feeling that I was incapable of making my living, the eternal life of heaven. I've always remained little, therefore, having no other occupation but to gather flowers, the flowers of love and sacrifice and offering them to God in order to please Him.

To be little is not attributing to oneself the virtues that one practices, not believing oneself capable of anything, but to recognize that God places this treasure in the hands of His little child to be used when necessary; but it remains always God's treasure. Finally, it is not to become discouraged over one's faults, for children fall often, but they are too little to hurt themselves very much.

Said to Mother Agnes of Jesus, August 6, 1897

O Lord,
All our powers of body and spirit,
every gift both natural and supernatural,
outward and inward,
comes as a blessing from You,
and reveals Your goodness, generosity and love,
for You have given us all that is good.
You know what is best to give each one;
and since it is clear to You what each one's merits are,
it is for You and not for us to decide why one has less
and another more.
And so, O Lord God, I can even consider it a great blessing
if I do not have much to bring me praise
and glory from man;
for when one does not have much,
he can look at his poverty and worthlessness,

and far from feeling burdened and sorrowful and dejected,
he can feel comforted and glad,
for it is the poor and humble and despised in the eyes of
the world that You have chosen, O God,
to be familiar members of your household.

The Imitation of Christ, Book 3, XXII, 126

Take Refuge As a Little Child

Whoever believes that Jesus is the Christ
is a child of God,
and whoever loves the father
loves the son.
In this way we know that
we love God's children,
when we love God and keep his commandments.
This is what the love of God is:
keeping his commandments.
Nor are his commandments burdensome,
because every child of God
overcomes the world.
And this is the victory that has overcome the world—
our faith.

1 John 5:1–4

I take refuge in my title, "a little child." Little children never realize all that their words imply, but if their father or mother were to come to the throne and inherit great riches, loving their little ones more than they love themselves, they would not hesitate to give them everything they want. They would be foolishly lavish just to please them, and go even as far as weakness. Well, I am a child of Holy Church, and the Church is a Queen, because she is espoused to You, the King of Kings.

My heart does not yearn for riches or for glory, not even the glory of Heaven; that belongs by rights to my brothers, the angels and saints. Mine will be the reflection of that glory which shines upon my Mother's brow.

No! what I ask for is love. Only one thing, my Jesus, to love You.

Striking deeds are forbidden me. I cannot preach the Gospel; I cannot shed my blood, but what matter? My brothers do it for me, while I, a little child, stay close beside the royal throne, and love for those who are fighting.

Love proves itself by deeds, and how shall I prove mine?...I can prove my love only by scattering flowers, that is to say, by never letting slip a single little sacrifice, a single glance, a single word; by making profit of the very smallest actions, by doing them all for love.

The Story of a Soul, XI, 158

Good Jesus,
carry me away,
part me from the transient comfort of created things,
for nothing that is created
can assuage and satisfy my longing.
Join me to Yourself
in the unbreakable bond of love,
for You alone can satisfy the yearning of my love,
and all things are meaningless without You.
                    The Imitation of Christ, Book 3, XXIII, 130

To Be His, One Must Be Small

The greater you are, the more humbly you should behave,
and then you will find favor with the Lord;
for great though the power of the Lord is,
he accepts the homage of the humble.
Do not try to understand things that are too difficult for you,
or try to discover what is beyond your powers.
Concentrate on what has been assigned to you,
you have no need to worry over mysteries.
Do not meddle with matters that are beyond you;
what you have been taught already exceeds the scope
of the human mind.
                                    Ecclesiasticus 3:18–23

To be His, one must be small, small as a drop of dew! Oh! how few souls there are that aspire to stay so small. "But," say they, "the river and the brook are surely more useful than the dewdrop? What does it do? It is good for nothing, save to give a few moments' refreshment to a flower of the fields which is today and tomorrow is no more."

They are right, of course: the dewdrop is good for no more than that; but they do not know the wild Flower which has chosen to dwell in our land of exile and remain here during the short night of this life. If they knew it, they would understand the rebuke Jesus gave Martha long ago (Luke 10:41). Our Beloved has no need of our fine thoughts—has He not His angels, His legions of heavenly spirits, whose knowledge infinitely surpasses that of the greatest geniuses of our sad earth?

So it is not intellect or talents that Jesus has come upon earth to seek. He became the Flower of the fields solely to show us how He loves simplicity....What a privilege to be called to so high a mission!...but to respond to it how simple one must remain.

Letter to Céline, April 25, 1893

O Lord,
All the glory of men,
all the honors of this world, all earthly rank,
beside Your eternal glory, are foolishness and unreality.

O God, my truth, my mercy,
O Blessed Trinity,
to You alone be blessing and honor and power and glory,
throughout endless generations.

The Imitation of Christ, Book 3, XL, 150

Love Shines Out Through Little Souls

Yahweh, my heart is not haughty,
I do not set my sights too high.
I have taken no part in great affairs,
in wonders beyond my scope.
No, I hold myself in quiet and silence,
like a little child in its mother's arms,
like a little child, so I keep myself.

Psalm 131:1–2

It pleases Him to create great saints, who may be compared with the lilies or the rose; but He has also created little ones who must be content to be daisies or violets nestling at His feet to delight His eyes when He should choose to look at them. The happier they are to be as He wills, the more perfect they are.

I saw something further; that Our Lord's love shines out just as much through a little soul who yields completely to His Grace as it does through the greatest. True love is shown in self-abasement, and if everyone were like the saintly doctors who adorn the Church, it would seem that God had not far enough to stoop when He came to them. But He has, in fact, created the child who knows nothing and can only make feeble cries; and the poor savage with only the natural law to guide him; and it is to hearts such as these that He stoops. What delights Him is the simplicity of these flowers of the field, and by stooping so low to them, He shows how infinitely great He is. Just as the sun shines equally on the cedar and the little flower, so the Divine Sun shines equally on everyone, great and small. Everything is ordered for their good, just as in nature the seasons are so ordered that the smallest daisy comes to bloom at its appointed time.

The Story of a Soul, I, 2

My Lord and my God,
You are good above all that is good.
You alone are most high, most mighty,
most sufficient, most complete;
You alone are full of sweetness,
of comfort, of beauty and love;
You alone are exalted and glorious above all things;
and in You all good things have their perfect existence,
as they always have done and as they always shall.
Therefore I am not satisfied by anything You give me
that is not Yourself,
nor by any promise or revelation
that does not let me see You or receive You fully.
My heart cannot really rest or find full satisfaction
unless it rests in You.

The Imitation of Christ, Book 3, XXI, 124

A Little, Short, New Way to Heaven

Rejoice with Jerusalem,
be glad for her, all you who love her!
Rejoice, rejoice with her,
all you who mourned her!...
For Yahweh says this:
Look, I am going to send peace flowing over her like a river
and like a stream in spate the glory of the nations.
You will be suckled, carried at her hip and fondled in her lap.
As a mother comforts a child, so shall I comfort you;
you will be comforted in Jerusalem.

Isaiah 66:10,12–13

You know that I have always wanted to be a saint; but compared with real saints I know perfectly well that I am no more like them than a grain of sand trodden beneath the feet of passers-by is like a mountain with its summit lost in the clouds.

Instead of allowing this to discourage me, I say to myself: "God would never inspire me with desires which cannot be realized, so in spite of my littleness, I can hope to be a saint. I could never grow up. I must put up with myself as I am, full of imperfections, but I will find a little way to Heaven, very short and direct, an entirely new way."

We live in the age of inventions now, and the wealthy no longer have to take the trouble to climb the stairs; they take the elevator. That is what I must find, an elevator to take me straight up to Jesus, because I am too little to climb the steep stairway of perfection.

So I searched the Scriptures for some hint of my desired means until I came upon these words from the lips of Eternal Wisdom: "Whosoever is a little one, let him come to Me" (Proverbs 9:4). I went closer to God, feeling sure that I was on the right path, but as I wanted to know what He would do to a "little one" I continued my search. This is what I found: "You shall be carried at the breasts and upon the knees; as one whom the mother caresseth, so will I comfort you" (Isaiah 66:12,13). My heart had never been moved by such tender and consoling words before!

Your arms, My Jesus, are the elevator which will take me up to heaven. There is no need for me to grow up; on the contrary, I must stay little, and become more and more so.

The Story of a Soul, IX, 109

Lord,
Even if we find this earthly life a burden,
it has been made a source of merit through Your grace;
and Your example and the traces left by the saints
who followed You have made it brighter
and easier for weaker people to bear.
What endless thanks I owe You
for graciously showing me and all who believe in You
the straight good road to Your eternal kingdom.
For the life You lived is our life,
and by holy patience we travel towards You,
our reward at the end of the journey.

The Imitation of Christ, Book 3, XVIII, 120

In Utter Littleness, Gaze Upon Love

Bless Yahweh, my soul,
from the depths of my being, his holy Name;
bless Yahweh, my soul,
never forget his acts of kindness.
He forgives all your offenses,
cures all your diseases,
he redeems your life from the abyss,
crowns you with faithful love and tenderness;
he contents you with good things all your life,
renews your youth like an eagle's.

Psalm 103:1–5

My only Friend, why not reserve such boundless aspirations to great souls, souls like eagles, who can wing their way to the stars? I am no eagle, only a little fledgling which has not yet lost its down, yet the eagles' heart is mine, and the eagles' eyes, and despite my utter littleness I dare to gaze upon the Sun of Love, burning to take my flight to Him. I long to fly and imitate the eagles, but all I can do is flutter my small wings. I am not strong enough to fly.

What will become of me? Must I die of sorrow at finding myself so helpless? Never! It will not trouble me in the very least. Surrendering myself with daring confidence, I shall simply stay gazing at my Sun until I die. Nothing will frighten me, neither wind nor rain, and should the Star of Love be blotted out by heavy clouds so that nothing but the night of this life seems to exist, then will be the time for perfect joy, the moment to push my confidence to the furthest bounds; I shall take good care to stay just where I am, quite certain that beyond the somber clouds my beloved Sun is shining still!...I am so happy, my dear Star, to feel little and frail in Your presence, and my heart remains at peace. I know that all the eagles in Your heavenly court look compassionately down on me, protecting and defending me, putting to flight the demon vultures who seek to prey on me.

The Story of a Soul, XI, 160

> *Lord,*
> *I cannot do this by nature—*
> *Make me able to do it by grace.*
> *You know that I am not able to endure very much,*
> *and that I am downcast by the slightest difficulty.*
> *Grant that for Your sake*
> *I may come to love and desire any hardship*
> *that puts me to the test.*
> *The Imitation of Christ, Book 3, XIX, 122*

Love Chooses a Multitude of Little Souls

For my part, this is my covenant with them, says Yahweh.
My spirit with which I endowed you,
and my words which I put in your mouth,
will not leave your mouth,

or the mouths of your children,
or the mouths of your children's children,
says Yahweh,
henceforth and for ever.

Isaiah 59:21

I know I am no more than a helpless little child, yet, my Jesus, it is my very helplessness which makes me dare to offer myself as a victim to Your love!

In bygone days, only pure and spotless victims were acceptable to Almighty God; to satisfy Divine Justice, they must be perfect. But now the law of fear is superseded by the law of love, and love has chosen me as a victim, frail and imperfect as I am. It is surely a worthy choice for love to make, since to be wholly satisfied it must stoop down to nothingness and turn that nothingness to fire.

I know, my God, that "Love is repaid by love alone" (Saint John of the Cross) and so I have sought and found a way to ease my heart by giving love for love.

The Story of a Soul, XI, 157

If only, my Jesus, I could tell all little souls about Your ineffable condescension!

I feel that if, supposing the impossible, You could find a soul more weak than mine, You would delight in lavishing upon it far more graces still, so long as it abandoned itself with boundless confidence to Your infinite mercy.

But why this desire to tell others the secrets of Your love?

Can You not, Yourself, reveal to others what You have revealed to me? I know You can, and I beg You to do so; I implore You, cast Your eyes upon a multitude of little souls; choose out in this world, I beg of You, a legion of little victims worthy of Your love.

The Story of a Soul, XI, 161

Heavenly Father and Father of my Lord Jesus Christ,
I bless You because You have in your mercy
remembered so poor a creature as me.
O merciful Father, the God who gives all encouragement,
I bring You my thanks
because You send Your comfort to encourage me
when I deserve no comfort at all.
O Father with the only-begotten Son
and the Holy Spirit the Comforter,
I bless you always and give You the glory for ever.
Dear Lord and God! O Holy One, O Lover of my soul!
when You come to my heart,
all that is within me will leap up for joy.

The Imitation of Christ, Book 3, V, 101

A Small Grain of Sand, an Atom

Do not love the world
or what is in the world.
If anyone does love the world,
the love of the Father finds no place in him,
because everything there is in the world—

21

> disordered bodily desires,
> disordered desires of the eyes,
> pride in possession—
> is not from the Father
> but is from the world.
> And the world, with all its disordered desires,
> is passing away.
> But whoever does the will of God
> remains for ever.
>
> *1 John 2:15–17*

If you knew how great is my wish to be indifferent to the things of this world! What matter all created beauties to me?

Possessing them, I should be utterly unhappy, my heart would be so empty!…It's incredible how big a thing my heart seems when I consider the world's treasures…since all of them massed together could not content it…but how small a thing it seems when I consider Jesus! I want to love Him so!…To love Him more than He has ever been loved!—My sole desire is to do the will of Jesus always, to dry the tears that sinners cause Him to shed.…Oh! I want Jesus to have no pain the day of my espousals, I wish I could convert all the sinners on earth and bring all the souls in purgatory to heaven!

The Lamb of Jesus[1] will laugh to see such a wish from the small grain of sand!…I know that it is foolishness, but still I wish that it could be so, that Jesus might not have a single tear to shed.

---

[1]Thérèse loved to call her sister by this symbolic name.

Pray that the grain of sand may become an atom, which only the eyes of Jesus can see.

Letter to Sister Agnes of Jesus, January 8(?), 1889

O Lord,
grant me heavenly wisdom,
so that I may learn above all things to seek You
and to find You,
above all things to delight in You
and love You;
and to value everything else according to its place
in Your wise plan.

The Imitation of Christ, Book 3, XXVII, 134

Lose Your Little Nothingness in His All

It is, then, about my weaknesses
that I am happiest of all to boast,
so that the power of Christ may rest upon me;
and that is why I am glad of weakness,
insults, constraints, persecutions and distress
for Christ's sake.
For it is when I am weak that I am strong.

2 Corinthians 12:9–10

Y̲ou must not forget Jesus is All, so you must lose your little nothingness in His infinite All and from now on think only of that uniquely lovable All....Nor must you desire to see the fruits of your efforts, Jesus likes to keep, for Himself alone, these little nothings which console Him....You are wrong if you think little Thérèse always marches with ardor along the way of virtue, she is weak, very weak; every day she experiences it afresh; but Jesus delights to teach her, as He taught Saint Paul, the science of glorying in one's infirmities (2 Corinthians 12:5); that is a great grace, and I beg Jesus to teach it to you, for in it alone is found peace and rest for the heart. Seeing yourself so worthless, you wish no longer to look at yourself, you look only at the sole Beloved!

For my part I know no other means to arrive at perfection save love....Love, how evidently our heart is made for that!... Sometimes I try to find another word to express love, but on this earth of exile words are impotent to render all the vibrations of the soul, so one must rest satisfied with the single word Love!

But upon whom shall our poor love-famished heart pour itself out?...Ah! Who shall be great enough for that?...Can a human being comprehend it...still more, can he return it?... There is but one being who can comprehend the depths of the word Love!...None but our Jesus can return us infinitely more than we give Him.

Letter to Marie Guérin, July 1890

Behold my God and my All.
What more can I want?
What more blessed thing can I desire?

How full of sweetness and delight these words seem
to a man who loves the Word,
and not the world and what the world has to offer.
My God and my All!
No other words are needed if a man understands;
and if he loves, there is joy in repeating them often.
The Imitation of Christ, Book 3, XXXIV, 142

Be Poor, With Nowhere to Lay Your Head

He said to them,
"In truth I tell you,
there is no one who has left house, wife, brothers, parents or
children for the sake of the kingdom of God
who will not receive many times as much in this present age
and, in the world to come, eternal life."

Luke 18:29–30

Like Zacchaeus we "have climbed up into a tree to see Jesus" (Luke 19:4)....So we could say with Saint John of the Cross: "All is mine, all is for me; the earth is mine, the heavens are mine, God is mine and the Mother of my God is mine"....What a mystery is our greatness in Jesus!...And now, what new truth is He going to teach us? Has He not taught us everything? Listen to what He tells us: "Make haste and come down, for this day I must abide in thy house" (Luke 19:5). Good! Jesus tells us to come down! But where must we come down?...Let me tell you where now we must go with Jesus. At one time the Jews asked our Divine Savior: "Master, where dwellest Thou?" (John 1:38). And He answered them: "The foxes have their holes and the birds of the air their nests but I have not where to lay my head" (Matthew 8:20). That is where we must come down, if we are to serve as a dwelling for Jesus: we must be so poor that we have not where to lay our head….

You realize that I am talking of the interior dwelling….Jesus wants us to receive Him in our hearts; by now, doubtless, they are empty of creatures; but alas! I feel that mine is not wholly empty of me, which is why Jesus tells me to come down.

Letter to Céline, October 19, 1892

Lord,
It is a great honor and great glory to serve You,
and for Your sake to reject all things as worthless.
For those who of their own free will
submit to Your holy service
will receive great grace;
those who reject all the delights of this physical life
for love of You
will find the sweet comfort of the Holy Spirit;
and those who for Your sake step out upon the narrow way
and cease to care about anything in this world,
will know great inner freedom.

The Imitation of Christ, Book 3, X, 110

God Upholds Little Souls

Jesus said to them,
"In truth I tell you,
tax collectors and prostitutes are making their way
into the kingdom of God before you.
For John came to you, showing the way of uprightness,
but you did not believe him,
and yet the tax collectors and prostitutes did."

Matthew 21:31–32

Never seek after what seems great to the eyes of creatures. Solomon, the wisest king there ever was upon the earth, having considered all the various labors that occupy men under the sun—painting, sculpture, all the arts—realized that all these things were subject to envy and cried out that they are nought but "vanity and affliction of spirit" (Ecclesiastes 1:14).

The one thing that is not envied is the last place; the last place is the one thing that is not vanity and affliction of spirit.

Yet "the way of man is not his own" (Jeremiah 10:23) and sometimes we surprise ourselves by wanting something that catches the eye. Then we must number ourselves humbly with the imperfect, see ourselves as little souls which God must uphold from instant to instant. The moment He sees us convinced of our nothingness, He reaches out His hand: if we still want to try some great thing, even under color of zeal, the good Jesus leaves us to ourselves: "If I said: My foot is moved; thy mercy, O Lord, assisted me" (Psalm 94:18). Yes, it is enough if we humble ourselves and bear our imperfections patiently: that is true sanctity. Let us take each other's hand and run to the last place, no one will dispute with us.

Letter to Sister Geneviève, June 7, 1897

O Spring of never-ceasing love,
what shall I say of You?
How can I forget You,
when you stooped to remember me
though I was sick and lost.
This is the great and wonderful thing—
that You are prepared
to take such a destitute and unworthy creature
into Your service,
and to add him to Your beloved household.
Why, everything I have,
everything by which I serve You,
is Yours already.

The Imitation of Christ, Book 3, X, 110

A Little Lamp Can Cause a Fire

Asked by the Pharisees
when the kingdom of God was to come,
he gave them this answer,
"The coming of the kingdom of God
does not admit of observation
and there will be no one to say,

Joyful Humility

'Look, it is here!
Look, it is there!'
For look, the kingdom of God is among you."
Luke 17:20–21

Sister Marie of the Eucharist wanted to light the candles for a procession; she had no matches; however, seeing the little lamp which was burning in front of the relics, she approached it. Alas, it was half out; there remained only a feeble glimmer on its blackened wick. She succeeded in lighting her candle from it, and with this candle, she lighted those of the whole community. It was, therefore, the half-extinguished little lamp which had produced all these beautiful flames which, in their turn, could produce an infinity of others and even light the whole universe. Nevertheless, it would always be the little lamp which would be first cause of all this light. How could the beautiful flames boast of having produced this fire, when they themselves were lighted with such a small spark?

It is the same with the Communion of Saints. Very often, without our knowing it, the graces and lights that we receive are due to a hidden soul, for God wills that the saints communicate grace to each other through prayer with great love, with a love much greater than that of a family, and even the most perfect family on earth....In heaven we shall not meet with indifferent glances, because all the elect will discover that they owe to each other the graces that merited the crown for them.

Said to Mother Agnes of Jesus, July 15, 1897

Good Jesus,
enlighten me with the brightness of the inward light,
and from the hiding places of my heart
bring out all that is dark.
Curb the many wanderings of my thoughts,
and crush the temptations that press me so hard.
Fight powerfully for me,
drive from their strongholds the evil desires
that lurk to entrap me;
then there will be "peace within thy ramparts" (Psalm
122:7)
and abundant praise will re-echo in the sacred temple
that my purified heart shall become.

The Imitation of Christ, Book 3, XXIII, 129

Realizing My Nothingness More

He spoke the following parable
to some people who prided themselves on being upright
and despised everyone else.
"Two men went up to the Temple to pray, one a Pharisee,
the other a tax collector.
The Pharisee stood there and said this prayer to himself,
'I thank you, God, that I am not grasping, unjust, adulterous
like everyone else,
and particularly that I am not like this tax collector here.
I fast twice a week; I pay tithes on all I get.'
The tax collector stood some distance away,

not daring even to raise his eyes to heaven;
but he beat his breast and said,
'God, be merciful to me, a sinner.'
This man, I tell you, went home again justified;
the other did not.
For everyone who raises himself up will be humbled,
but anyone who humbles himself will be raised up."

Luke 18:9–14

I f I were to say to myself: I have acquired a certain virtue, and I am certain I can practice it....this would be relying upon my own strength, and when we do this, we run the risk of falling into the abyss. However, I will have the right of doing stupid things up until my death, if I am humble and if I remain little. Look at little children: they never stop breaking things, tearing things, falling down, and they do this even while loving their parents very, very much. When I fall in this way, it makes me realize my nothingness more, and I say to myself: What would I do, and what would I become, if I were to rely upon my own strength?

Said to Mother Agnes of Jesus, August 7, 1897

Lord,
I will confess my weakness to You.
Often it is such a small thing
that makes me downcast and sad.
I make up my mind to act boldly,
and when a temptation comes,

I suffer anguish out of all proportion.
Sometimes it is quite an unimportant thing
that gives rise to serious temptation;
and just when I think I am safe for a while,
before I realize what is happening,
a little gust of wind almost has me over.
Great God of Israel, lover of faithful souls,
take pity on the labors and sorrows of Your servant,
and be at his side wherever he goes.
The Imitation of Christ, Book 3, XX, 122

God Shows Me My Weakness

It is God who said: "Let light shine out of darkness,"
that has shone into our hearts to enlighten them
with the knowledge of God's glory,
the glory on the face of Christ.
But we hold this treasure in pots of earthenware,
so that the immensity of the power is God's and not our own.
We are subjected to every kind of hardship,
but never distressed;
we see no way out but we never despair;
we are pursued but never cut off;
knocked down, but still have some life in us;
always we carry with us in our body the death of Jesus
so that the life of Jesus, too, may be visible in our body.
2 Corinthians 4:6–10

I understand very well why Saint Peter fell. Poor Peter, he was relying upon himself instead of relying only on God's strength. I conclude from this experience that if I said to myself: "O my God, You know very well I love You too much to dwell upon one single thought against the faith," my temptations would become more violent and I would certainly succumb to them.

I'm very sure that if Saint Peter had said humbly to Jesus: "Give me the grace, I beg You, to follow You even to death," he would have received it immediately.

I'm very certain that Our Lord didn't say any more to His Apostles through His instructions and His physical presence than He says to us through His good inspirations and His grace. He could have said to Saint Peter: "Ask me for the strength to accomplish what you want." But no, He didn't because He wanted to show him his weakness, and because, before ruling the Church that is filled with sinners, he had to experience for himself what man is able to do without God's help.

Before Peter fell, our Lord had said to him: "And once you are converted, strengthen your brethren" (Luke 22:32). This means: Convince them of the weakness of human strength through your own experience.

Said to Mother Agnes of Jesus, August 7, 1897

Beloved Father,
what shall I say?
Troubles hem me in from every side.
Save me from undergoing this hour of trial—
and yet I have only reached this hour of trial

that I may undergo it and bring glory to Your Name;
for it is You who shall deliver me
when I have been brought low.
O Lord, be willing to rescue me, for I am helpless;
what can I do, where can I go without You.
Grant me patience, Lord, on this occasion too.
Help me, O my God,
and I shall not be afraid,
however heavy my burden.

The Imitation of Christ, Book 3, XXIV, 135

2

Bold Confidence in God's Mercy and Loving Kindness

Do not let your hearts be troubled.
You trust in God, trust also in me....
Peace I bequeath to you, my own peace I give you,
a peace which the world cannot give, this is my gift to you.
Do not let your hearts be troubled or afraid.
                                                    John 14:1,27

My way is all of trust and love.
I don't understand souls who fear so tender a Friend.

                          From a letter to Père Roulland, May 9, 1897

If Jesus is with you, no enemy can harm you.
The man who finds Jesus finds a wonderful treasure,
a treasure beyond all other treasures.
                          The Imitation of Christ, Book 2, VIII

Introduction

Weak, little, powerless children need a friend who can supply all their wants. As they grow in littleness, that friend can do more and more for them. Jesus turned to His heavenly Father for every need, as a Son with absolute trust and confidence in His Father's loving, constant attention. "Is there anyone among you would hand his son a stone when he asked for bread?...[H]ow much more will your Father in heaven give good things to those who ask him!" (Matthew 7:9,11b).

God's willingness and ability to give to His children is limitless. He has shown that to be so in giving His only Son to us; Jesus promised that "the Father will give you anything you ask him in my name" (John 15:16b). He stressed this willingness: "If you ask for anything in my name, I will do it" (John 14:14). So the child of God can have unbounded confidence in God's loving mercy and kindness, and even be bold in dependency and requests. Thérèse made her own the saying of Saint John of the Cross: "One obtains from God what one hopes for." Our hopes and expectations in the love of God should be limitless, like His willingness.

"I hope as much from the good God's justice as from His mercy," wrote Thérèse, and "How can He purify in the flames of purgatory souls consumed in the fires of divine love?" She simply reflected the teaching of John the beloved Apostle, who said, "In love there is no room for fear" (1 John 4:18a).

If the child of God has full and fearless trust and confidence in Him, He will not measure His gifts and assistance in return. "When we accept our disappointment at our failures, God immediately returns to us," said Thérèse. And we have Jesus' assurance that no one who believes in and follows Him will be judged, for their Father sent His Son not to judge but to save sinners (John 3:17,18).

I Know What to Believe About His Mercy and Love

Then he turned to the woman and said to Simon,
"You see this woman? I came into your house,
and you poured no water over my feet,
but she has poured out her tears over my feet
and wiped them away with her hair.
You gave me no kiss, but she has been
covering my feet with kisses ever since I came in.
You did not anoint my head with oil, but she has
anointed my feet with ointment.
For this reason I tell you that her sins,
many as they are, have been forgiven her,
because she has shown such great love.
It is someone who is forgiven little who shows little love."
Then he said to her, "Your sins are forgiven."
Those who were with Him at table
began to say to themselves, "Who is this man,
that even forgives sins?" But he said to the woman,
"Your faith has saved you; go in peace."

Luke 7:44–50

Bold Confidence

I have only to glance at the Gospels; at once this fragrance from the life of Jesus reaches me, and I know which way to run; to the lowest, not the highest place! Leaving the Pharisee to push himself forward, I pray humbly like the Publican, but full of confidence.

Yet most of all I follow the example of Mary Magdalene, my heart captivated by her astonishing, or rather, loving audacity, which so won the heart of Jesus. It is not only because I have been preserved from mortal sin that I fly to Jesus with such confidence and love; even if I had all the crimes possible on my conscience, I am sure I should lose none of my confidence. Heartbroken with repentance, I would simply throw myself into my Savior's arms, for I know how much He loves the prodigal son. I have heard what He said to Mary Magdalene, to the woman taken in adultery, and to the Samaritan woman. No one can make me frightened any more, because I know what to believe about His mercy and love; I know that in a twinkling of an eye all those thousands of sins would be consumed as a drop of water cast into a blazing fire.

The Story of a Soul, X, 148

God meets the penitent with a loving holy kiss.
O Lord, when the humble repentance of sinners
is offered up before You,
You take pleasure in the sacrifice,
its perfume is sweeter than incense as it rises up before
You. This is the precious ointment that
You wished to have poured on Your holy feet,

for a heart that is humbled and contrite
You have never disdained.
There is the place of refuge from our enemy's furious glance;
there is the place where every mark and stain
is cleansed and washed away.

The Imitation of Christ, Book 3, LII 169

God Is Even Kinder Than You Think

"Let the little children come to me; do not stop them;
for it is to such as these that the kingdom of God belongs.
In truth I tell you, anyone who does not welcome
the kingdom of God like a little child will never enter it."
Then he embraced them, laid his hands on them and gave
them his blessing.

Mark 10:14–16

I assure you that God is even kinder than you think. He is satisfied with a look, a sigh of love....I have realized that all one has to do is take Jesus by the heart. Consider a small child who has displeased his mother, by flying into a rage or perhaps disobeying her; if he sulks in a corner and screams in fear of punishment, his mother will certainly not forgive his fault. But if he comes to her with outstretched arms, smiling and saying, "Kiss me, I won't do it again," surely his mother will immediately press him tenderly to her heart, forgetting all that he has done.

Letter to Léonie, July 12, 1896

Truly, it is beyond man's power to tell the loving-kindness
that You pour out on those who love You,
when You let them see Yourself.
And I see the sweetness of Your love in this above all things:
when I did not exist, You created me;
when I wandered far from You, You brought me back
in order to make me Your servant,
and then commanded me to give You my love.

The Imitation of Christ, Book 3, X, 109

Be Simple With the Good God

People even brought babies to him, for him to touch them;
but when the disciples saw this they scolded them.
But Jesus called the children to him and said,
"Let the little children come to me, and do not stop them;
for it is to such as these that the kingdom of God belongs.
In truth I tell you, anyone who does not welcome
the kingdom of God like a little child will never enter it."

Luke 18:15–17

He has long forgotten your infidelities, only your desires for perfection are present to give joy to His heart....For those who love Him and, after each discourteous act, cast themselves into His arms and ask pardon, Jesus is vibrant with joy. He says to His angels what the prodigal son's father said to his servants: "Put on him the first robe, put a ring on his hand, and let us make merry." Ah! Brother, how little are Jesus' kindness and merciful love realized! It is true that, to enjoy His riches, we must humble ourselves, see our own nothingness, which is what many souls will not do; but, little Brother, you do not act like them, so the way of simple loving confidence is indeed the way for you. I would have you to be simple with the good God.

Letter to Abbé Bellière, July 26, 1897

O Lord God,
Crowds of friends will be no use,
and strong supporters will have no power to help;
wise counsellors will not give good advice
and learned books will bring no comfort;
no precious substance will liberate,
no lovely hidden spot protect,
unless You draw near: help, comfort and console me,
teach me and keep me safe.
For all the things which seem to contribute
to our peace and blessedness
are ineffective and can bring no happiness without You.
You are the goal of all that is good,
You are the true sublimity of life, true depth of wisdom;
and your servants find their most lasting comfort
if beyond all things they rest their hopes in You.
I look to You; I trust in You,
my God and merciful Father.

The Imitation of Christ, Book 3, LIX, 183

Love Alone Can Make Us Pleasing to God

At this time the disciples came to Jesus and said,
"Who is the greatest in the kingdom of Heaven?"
So he called a little child to him whom he set among them.
Then he said, "In truth I tell you, unless you change
and become like little children you will never enter
the Kingdom of Heaven.
And so, the one who makes himself as little as this little child
is the greatest in the kingdom of Heaven."

Matthew 18:1–4

L ove alone can make us pleasing to God, so I desire no other treasure. Jesus has chosen to show me the only way which leads to the Divine Furnace of love; it is the way of childlike self-surrender, the way of a child who sleeps, afraid of nothing, in its father's arms. "Whosoever is a little one, let him come unto Me" (Proverbs 9:4), says the Holy Spirit through the lips of Solomon, and the same Spirit of Love tells us also that "to him that is little, mercy is granted" (Wisdom 6:7).

In His name the prophet Isaiah has revealed that on the Last Day "the Lord shall feed His flock like a shepherd; He shall gather together the lambs with His arm and shall take them up into His bosom" (Isaiah 40:11). As if all this were not proof enough, the same prophet, piercing the depths of eternity with eyes inspired, cried out in the name of Our Lord: "You shall be carried at the breasts, and upon the knees shall they caress you. As one whom the mother caresseth, so will I comfort you" (Isaiah 66:12–13).

One can only remain silent, one can only weep for gratitude and love, after words like these. If only everyone weak and imperfect like me felt as I do, no one would despair of reaching the heights of love, for Jesus does not ask for glorious deeds. He asks only for self-surrender and for gratitude.

The Story of a Soul, XI, 151

Most kind Jesus,
grant me Your grace to be at my side
and share my labors and remain with me right to the end.
Grant that it may always be my longing and desire
to do what is acceptable and pleasing to You.
May Your will become mine,
and my will always follow Yours in perfect harmony.
I rest in You, the highest, the everlasting Good,
and even as I lie down, sleep comes,
and with sleep tranquillity.

The Imitation of Christ, Book 3, XV, 117

Always Have Confidence in God

No need to remember past events,
no need to think about what was done before....
Thus says Yahweh who made you,
who formed you in the womb; he will help you.
Do not be afraid, Jacob my servant,
Jeshurun whom I have chosen.

Bold Confidence

For I shall pour out water on the thirsty soil,
and streams on the dry ground.
I shall pour out my spirit on your descendants,
my blessing on your offspring.

Isaiah 43:18; 44:2–3

One could believe that it is because I haven't sinned that I have such a great confidence in God. Really tell them, Mother, that if I had committed all possible crimes, I would always have the same confidence; I feel this whole multitude of sins would be like a drop of water thrown into a fiery furnace. You will then tell the story about the converted sinner who died of love; souls will understand immediately, for it is such a striking example of what I'm trying to say. However, these things cannot be expressed in words.

Saint Thérèse had previously told the story as follows:

It is related in the *Lives of the Fathers of the Desert* that one of them converted a women who was a public sinner, and whose evil life had scandalized the entire countryside. Touched by grace, that poor sinner followed the saint into the desert, there to carry out rigorous penance. On the first night of the journey, however, even before she had come to the place of her retreat, her earthly ties were snapped by the violence of her repentant love. At that very moment, the holy man saw her soul being carried by angels up to the very bosom of God. This is a striking example of what I mean but cannot express.

Said to Mother Agnes of Jesus, July 11, 1897

May all praise be Yours, O God,
for though I am unworthy of any good gift,
yet in Your generosity and infinite goodness
You never cease to bless even the ungrateful
and those who turn their backs on You
and wander far away.
Turn us back to Yourself,
so that we may be thankful, humble and loving;
for You are our salvation,
our boldness and our strength.

The Imitation of Christ, Book 3, VIII, 108

What Have I to Fear Then?

I have dispelled your acts of revolt like a cloud
and your sins like a mist.
Come back to me, for I have redeemed you....
Thus says Yahweh, your redeemer,
he who formed you in the womb.

Isaiah 44:22,24a

May I not sing with the psalmist that "the Lord is good, that his mercy endureth for ever"? (Psalm 117:1). It seems to me that if everyone received such graces, no one would dread Him but love Him with an unbounded love; for it is love rather than fear which leads us to avoid the smallest voluntary fault.

But then I realized that we cannot all be alike; there must be different kinds of holiness to glorify the divine perfections. To me He has manifested His Infinite Mercy, and it is in this shining armor that I gaze upon His other attributes which there appear all radiant with love, all, even justice.

What joy to remember that our Lord is just; that He makes allowances for all our shortcomings, and knows full well how weak we are. What have I to fear then? Surely the God of infinite justice who pardons the Prodigal Son with such mercy will be just with me "who am always with Him"? (Luke 15:31).

The Story of a Soul, VIII, 105

It is Your love that does this,
the love that from pure affection surrounds my path,
and comes to help me in my many needs,
that keeps me safe from danger
and rescues me from countless ills.
For by sinfully loving myself, I lost myself,
but by seeking You alone and loving You wholeheartedly
I have found both myself and You,
and by that love have been utterly humbled again;
for You show me kindness, O my Sweetest God,
beyond all that I deserve, beyond all I dare ask or hope.
The Imitation of Christ, Book 3, VIII, 108

The Way Is All of Trust and Love

Everyone whom the Father gives me will come to me;
I will certainly not reject anyone who comes to me,
because I have come from heaven, not to do my own will,
but to do the will of him who sent me.
Now the will of him who sent me is that I should lose nothing
of all that he has given to me,
but that I should raise it up on the last day....
No one can come to me unless drawn by the Father who sent
me,
and I will raise that person up on the last day.
It is written in the prophets. "They will all be taught by God";
everyone who has listened to the Father,
and learnt from him, comes to Me.

John 6:37–39,44–45

My way is all of trust and love, I don't understand souls who are afraid of so loving a Friend. Sometimes, when I read spiritual treatises, in which perfection is shown with a thousand obstacles in the way and a host of illusions round it, my poor little mind grows very soon weary. I close the learned book, which leaves my head muddled and my heart parched, and I take up the Holy Scripture. Then all seems luminous, a single word opens up infinite horizons to my soul, perfection seems easy; I see it is enough to realize one's nothingness and give oneself wholly, like a child, into the arms of the good God.

Leaving to great souls, great minds, the fine books I can't understand, I rejoice to be little, because "only children, and those like them, will be admitted to the heavenly banquet" (Matthew 19:14). I am so happy that "in the Kingdom of God there are so many mansions" (John 14:2), for if there were but the one, the description of which and the way to which seem incomprehensible, I could not get in.

Letter to Père Roulland, May 9, 1897

I am the One that in a moment can raise the humble mind
to more understanding of eternal truth
than if he had given ten years to study.
In My teaching there is no babble of words,
no confusion of opinions,
no arrogance of authority,
no conflict of argument.
To some I give a general message,
to others I say things meant only for them;
to certain people my sweet presence is known
in signs and symbols,
while to a few I reveal mysteries in dazzling light.
Books speak with one voice,
but not everyone learns the same from them;
for I am within a man, the Truth that teaches him—
I search his heart,
I know his thoughts,
I advance his actions,
and give to each what I think he should have.
The Imitation of Christ, Book 3, XLIII, 153

It Is Good to Feel Weak

Shout for joy, you heavens; earth, exult!
Mountains, break into joyful cries!
For Yahweh has consoled his people,
is taking pity on his afflicted ones.
Zion was saying, "Yahweh has abandoned me,
the Lord has forgotten me."
Can a woman forget the baby at the breast,
feel no pity for the child she has borne?
Even if these were to forget,
I shall not forget you.

Isaiah 49:13–15

I have my weaknesses also, but I rejoice in them. I don't always succeed either in rising above the nothings of this world; for example, I will be tormented by a foolish thing I said or did. Then I enter into myself, and I say: Alas, I'm still at the same place as I was formerly! But I tell myself this with great gentleness and without any sadness! It is so good to feel that one is weak and little!

Said to Mother Agnes of Jesus, July 5, 1897

God does not deceive you,
but you will be deceived if you trust too much to yourself.
God walks with simple people,
and reveals Himself to humble ones.

It is to those who become like children
that He gives understanding,
and He enlarges the faculties of minds that are pure,
but from those who are arrogant and inquisitive
He keeps His grace concealed.
Human understanding is weak and easily deceived,
but true faith cannot be led astray.
God who is eternal, infinite, supremely mighty,
does great and unfathomable things in heaven and in earth
and there is no understanding His wonderful works.
If the works of God could easily be grasped
by human understanding
they could not be called wonderful or too great for words.
The Imitation of Christ, Book 4, XVIII, 217

Compassion for Our Wretchedness

Be sincere of heart, be steadfast,
and do not be alarmed when disaster comes.
Cling to him and do not leave him,
so that you may be honored at the end of your days.
Whatever happens to you, accept it,
and in the uncertainties of your humble state, be patient,
since gold is tested in the fire,
and the chosen in the furnace of humiliation.
Trust him and he will uphold you,
follow a straight path and hope in him.

Ecclesiasticus 2:2–6

The Little Way

O f course no human life is free from faults; only the immaculate Virgin presents herself in absolute purity before God's Majesty. What a joy to remember she is our Mother! Since she loves us and knows our weakness, what have we to fear?

Letter to Père Roulland, May 9, 1897

I believe that the Blessed in Heaven have a great compassion for our wretchedness; they remember that when they were frail and mortal like us they committed the same faults, endured the same struggles, and their fraternal love becomes greater even than it was on earth, which is why they do not cease to protect us and pray for us.

Letter to Abbé Bellière, August 10, 1897

O Lord my God,
Remember that I am nothing, have nothing, can do nothing.
You alone are good and just and holy.
You can do all things;
You bestow all things and fill all things,
leaving only the sinner empty.
Do not forget Your pity;
fill my heart with Your grace,
since You do not wish what You have made to be left empty.
Teach me, Lord, to do Your will,
teach me to live humbly and worthily before You—
for You are my wisdom;
You know me utterly,

and knew me before the world was made
and before I was born in the world.

The Imitation of Christ, Book 3, III, 98

A Wind of Love, Faster Than Lightning

You respond to us with the marvels of your saving justice,
God our Savior, hope of the whole wide world,
even the distant islands.
By your strength you hold the mountains steady,
being clothed in power, you calm the turmoil of the seas,
the turmoil of their waves.
The nations are in uproar,
in panic those who live at the ends of the earth;
your miracles bring shouts of joy
to the gateways of morning and evening.

Psalm 65:5–8

I am not surprised that you can make nothing of what is happening in your soul. A little child all alone, at sea, in a boat lost amid the stormy waters—could it know whether it was close to port or far off? While it can still see the shore it started from, it knows how much way it has made; seeing the land further and further away, it cannot contain its childish joy. Oh, it says, I'll soon be at the end of my journey. But the further away the shore becomes, the vaster the ocean looks....Then the child's knowledge is reduced to nothing, it no longer knows where its boat is going. It does not know how to handle the helm; so the only thing it can do is let itself be borne along, let its sail go with the wind....The boat that bears it on is speeding with all sails set towards the port; the helm, which it cannot even see, does not lack a pilot. Jesus is there, sleeping as long ago in the Galilean fishermen's boat (Matthew 8:24). He sleeps...and it does not see Him, for night has come down upon the boat...it does not hear Jesus' voice....The wind is high...it hears the wind... it sees the darkness...and Jesus sleeps on. Yet if He awoke only for an instant, He would have but "to command the wind and the sea, and there would come a great calm" (Matthew 8:26), night would be brighter than day....Be sure, your boat is in the open sea, already perhaps very close to port. The wind of sorrows driving it is a wind of love, and that is a wind that goes faster than lightning.

Letter to Céline, July 23, 1893

Good Jesus...
Check the winds and the storms;
say to the sea "Be still,"
and "Do not blow" to the wind;
then there will be deep calm.
The light of Your presence,
the fulfillment of Your promise,
let these be my escort.
Shed Your light on the earth,
for until You enlighten me,
I am earth that is empty and waste.
Shed Your grace on me from above:

54

bathe my heart in the dew of heaven,
and bring in the waters of devotion,
so that the face of the earth may be watered,
and good fruit be produced, fruit that is the best.
The Imitation of Christ, Book 3, XXIII, 129

Jesus Must Be Our Reward

When they drew near the village to which they were going,
he made as if to go on; but they pressed him to stay with them
saying, "It is nearly evening and the day is almost over."
So he went in to stay with them....Now while he was with them
at table, he took the bread and said the blessing; then he broke
it and handed it to them. And their eyes were opened and
they recognized him; but he had vanished from their sight.
Then they said to each other, "Did not our hearts burn
within us as he talked to us on the road
and explained the scriptures to us?"

Luke 24:28–32

Ah! If Jesus had chosen to show Himself to all souls with His
ineffable gifts, surely not one would have spurned Him; but
He does not want us to love Him for His gifts; it is Himself that
must be our reward. To find a thing hidden, we must ourselves
be hidden; so our life must be a mystery! We must be like Jesus,
like Jesus whose look was hidden (Isaiah 53:3). "Do you want to
learn something that may serve you?" says the *Imitation:* "Love

to be ignored and accounted for nothing." And in another place: "After you have left everything, you must above all leave yourself; let one man boast of one thing, one of another; for you, place your joy only in the contempt of yourself."

May these words give peace to your soul....Jesus loves you with a love so great that if you saw it, you would be in an ecstasy of happiness of which you would die, but you do not see it and you suffer.

Soon Jesus "will arise to save all the small and humble of the earth." (Psalm 75:10).

Letter to Céline, August 2, 1893

Dear Lord and God!
O Holy One,
O Lover of my soul!
when You come to my heart, all that is within me
will leap for joy
You are my glory, the rejoicing of my heart.
You are my hope and my refuge in my hour of peril.
Yet I am still weak in love, imperfect in goodness,
and I need Your strength and comfort.
So visit me often and teach me by Your holy discipline;
free me from evil passions,
and cure my heart of its undisciplined emotions;
then I shall be healthy and clean within,
made fit for loving, strong for suffering,
steadfast for enduring.

The Imitation of Christ, Book 3, V, 101

The Smallest Thing Is Precious to Him

As the chosen of God, then, the holy people whom he loves,
you are to be clothed in heartfelt compassion, in generosity
and humility, gentleness and patience. Bear with one another;
forgive each other if one of you has a complaint against
another. The Lord has forgiven you; now you must do the
same. Over all these clothes, put on love, the perfect bond.
And may the peace of Christ reign in your hearts, because it
was for this that you were called together in one body.
Always be thankful.

Colossians 3:12–15

Jesus does not want us in repose to find His adorable presence. He hides, is wrapped in darkness; not thus did He act
toward the multitude of the Jews, for we see in the Gospel that
the people were uplifted when He spoke to them (Luke 19:48).
Jesus charmed feeble souls by His divine words. He was trying
to make them strong against the day of trial....But how small
was the number of Our Lord's friends, when He was silent before
His judges (Matthew 26:63)....Oh! What a melody for my heart
is that silence of Jesus....He makes Himself poor that we may
be able to do Him charity; He stretches out His hand to us like a
beggar, that upon the sunlit day of Judgment, when He appears
in His glory, He may be able to utter and we to hear the loving
words: "Come, blessed of my Father; for I was hungry and you
gave Me to eat: I was thirsty and you gave Me to drink: I was

a stranger and you took Me in; I was in prison, sick, and you came to Me" (Matthew 25:34–36).

It was Jesus Himself who uttered those words, it is He who wants our love, begs for it. He puts Himself, so to say, at our mercy. He wills to take nothing unless we give it to Him, and the smallest thing is precious in His divine eyes.

Letter to Céline, August 2, 1893

When you have received the spirit of ardor,
it is a good plan to think what it will be like
when the light goes away;
and when that happens, to remind yourself
that the light can return,
though I have taken it away for a time to teach you caution
and to glory Myself.
It often does you more good to be tested like this
than to have things always going the way you want them to.
The Imitation of Christ, Book 3, VII, 106

Do Not Be Afraid of Rising Too High

God of our ancestors, Lord of mercy,
who by your word have made the universe,
and in your wisdom have fitted human beings to rule
the creatures that you have made,
to govern the world in holiness and saving justice
and in honesty of soul to dispense fair judgment,
grant me Wisdom, consort of your throne,

and do not reject me from the number of your children.
For I am your servant, son of your serving maid, a feeble man,
with little time to live,
with small understanding of justice and the laws.
Indeed, were anyone perfect among the sons of men,
if he lacked the Wisdom that comes from you,
he would still count for nothing.

Wisdom 9:1–6

Consider the oaks of our countryside, how crooked they are; they thrust their branches to right and left, nothing checks them so they never reach a great height. On the other hand, consider the oaks of the forest, which are hemmed in on all sides, they see light only up above, so their trunk is free of all those shapeless branches which rob it of the sap needed to lift it aloft. It sees only heaven, so all its strength is turned in that direction, and soon it attains a prodigious height. In the religious life the soul like the young oak is hemmed in on all sides by its rule. All its movements are hampered, interfered with by the other trees....But it has light when it looks toward heaven, there alone it can rest its gaze, never upon anything below, it need not be afraid of rising too high.

Letter to Léonie, November 5, 1893

But think of the harvest from these labors, My son;
think of the end that will soon come,
and the very great reward to follow—
then you will not feel any burden,
but will experience strong comfort in your patience.

For in place of this insignificant will of yours
which you now resign of your own accord,
you will have your will in Heaven always.
There you will have everything you want,
everything you can desire.
The Imitation of Christ, Book 3, XLIX, 163

Full Sail on the Sea of Confident Love

Do not be afraid, for I am with you; do not be alarmed,
for I am your God.
I give you strength, truly I help you, truly I hold you firm
with my saving right hand....
The oppressed and needy search for water,
and there is none, their tongue is parched with thirst.
I, Yahweh, shall answer them,
I, the God of Israel, shall not abandon them.
Isaiah 41:10,17

That year the general retreat was a time of great grace. Normally I find a preached retreat very trying, and as I had suffered so much before, I fortified myself by a fervent novena. But this was different.

It was said that the Father was better at converting sinners than at directing religious. I must, then, be a great sinner, because God certainly used him to help me.

I had been undergoing all sorts of interior trials at this time, which I could not explain to anyone, yet here was someone who understood me perfectly, as though inspired by God, and my soul opened out completely. He launched me full sail upon that sea of confidence and love which had attracted me so much, but on which I had never dared to set out. He told me that my faults did not cause God sorrow, and added: "At this moment I stand in His place as far as you are concerned, and on His behalf I assure you that He is very satisfied with your soul."

How happy these consoling words made me! No one had ever told me before that faults did not pain God; this assurance filled me with joy, and made it possible to bear my exile patiently. My inmost thoughts had been echoed. For a long time I had felt sure that Our Lord was more tender than any mother, and I had sounded the depths of more than one mother's heart. I know from experience that a mother is always ready to forgive her child's little involuntary faults. No rebuke could have touched me half as much as a single kiss from you. Such is my nature that fear only keeps me back, while under the sway of love I not only advance—I fly!

The Story of a Soul, VIII, 97

What return shall I make to the Lord for this grace,
for His wonderful love?
I can do nothing that will please Him more than give Him
my whole heart,
and closely unite it to Him.
And then, when my soul is perfectly joined to God,
all that is within me will leap up for joy.

Then He will say to me,
"If you wish to be with Me, then it is My wish to be
with you."
And I shall reply to Him, "Lord, stay with me in
Your mercy.
I am very glad to be with You.
The one thing that I desire is for my heart
to be one with You."

The Imitation of Christ, Book 4, XIII, 210

3

Tranquil Trust in the Actions of God's Limitless Love

I shall ask the Father, and he will give you another Paraclete
to be with you for ever,
the Spirit of truth
whom the world can never accept
since it neither sees nor knows him;
but you know him, because he is with you, he is in you.

John 14:16–17

My director, Jesus, does not teach me to count my acts,
but to do everything for love, to refuse Him nothing,
to be pleased when He gives me a chance to prove to Him
that I love Him—
but all this in peace, in abandonment.

Letter to Céline, July 6, 1893

As a man grows in inward unity and simplicity,
he finds that more and more deep truths are made plain to him
without any effort,
because a Heaven-sent Light brings him understanding.

The Imitation of Christ, Book 1, III, 36

Introduction

To understand Saint Thérèse's "short, direct, new way," it is helpful to remember that in her time many Christians had a concept of God as severely judgmental and requiring appeasement of His justice. This view of the stern God can often lead the individual to be only too conscious of great guilt and to fear God's punishments. From this viewpoint, Christ's crucifixion was an awesome act of sacrificial satisfaction of God's justice on behalf of sinners. Hence, many of Thérèse's companions in her community, as elsewhere, offered themselves and their penances to God's justice, seeking to join Christ and imitate Him in deflecting punishment from sinners.

This response was not accepted by Thérèse, although she recognized the generosity and, indeed, the heroism of it. She was led to understand and stress the intense love which Jesus shows forth for us from the Cross, through which He reveals the God who is our Father having all the love, patience, forbearance and yearnings of a good parent. God is not vengeful and overbearing; He has only love, He is Love, for His children. They themselves cannot accumulate merit, being feeble and unable as weak children. But God Himself desires to do all for them, and did so in utter final fullness on the Cross.

"Our God of Kindness has willed to...show me once again what delight He takes in accomplishing the desires of souls that love Him alone," wrote Thérèse. In contrast to her companions, Thérèse offered herself totally to God's Love (without any fear of His justice) in order to draw all to Him in love. Seeking to satisfy Love with love, she echoes that Christian tradition which is rooted in the teachings of Saint John the Evangelist.

The lover seeks only the pleasure, the will, of the beloved. So, Thérèse desires only the totality of what is willed by her Beloved. Love not only casts out all fear, but it also has complete trust—a serene trust—in the Beloved who, being Love, can only will all that is good and best. "Love is always patient and kind...it does not take offense or store up grievances...it is always ready to make allowances, to trust, to hope" (1 Corinthians 13:4–5, 7).

Thérèse becomes no longer concerned by the continual failure of her own efforts to become perfect with the spiritual wholeness which God offers her. She knows, like a child asleep in its parent's arms, that the actions of limitless Love will alone achieve all. It is our part simply to stay turned to God, to long for His will to be done, to peacefully trust Him completely, and to allow Him to act on us and for us. "Jesus does everything, I do nothing."

Only Trust Will Bring Love

How blessed are the poor in spirit:
the kingdom of Heaven is theirs.
Blessed are the gentle:
they shall have the earth as inheritance.
Matthew 5:3–4

Tranquil Trust

What pleases Him is to see me love my littleness and poverty, the blind hope I have in His mercy....That is my sole treasure; why should not this treasure be yours?...

Are you not ready to suffer whatever the good God wants? I know well that you are; then, if you want to feel joy in suffering, to be drawn to it, what you seek is your own consolation, for when one loves a thing, the pain vanishes....Understand that to love Jesus, to be His victim of love, the weaker one is, without desires or virtues, the more apt one is for the operations of that consuming and transforming Love. The desire to be a victim is enough of itself, but one must consent to stay always poor and without strength, and that's the difficulty, for where are we to find the man truly poor in spirit? He must be sought afar, says the psalmist. He does not say we must look for him among great souls, but "afar," that is, in lowliness, nothingness. Ah! do let us stay very far from all that is brilliant, let us love our littleness, love to feel nothing, then we shall be poor in spirit, and Jesus will come for us, far off as we are, He will transform us in love's flames....Oh! how I wish I could make you realize what I mean!... It is trust, and nothing but trust, that must bring us to Love....Fear brings us only to Justice.

Letter to Sister Marie of the Sacred Heart, September 17, 1896

The voice of the Lord:
Let Me do what I want with you, since I know what is best.
Your thoughts are the thoughts of a man,
and you judge as your human emotions suggest.

The Disciple:
Lord, what You say is true—
You care for me more than I can ever care for myself,
and any man who will not leave all his care with You
will stand very insecurely.

The Imitation of Christ, Book 3, XVII, 119

All One Has to Do Is Love

He was still speaking to the crowds when suddenly
his mother and brothers were standing outside
and were anxious to have a word with him.
But to the man who told him this Jesus replied,
"Who is my mother? Who are my brothers?"
And stretching out his hand towards His disciples he said,
"Here are my mother and my brothers.
Anyone who does the will of my father in heaven
is my brother and sister and mother."

Matthew 12:46–50

"My thoughts are not your thoughts," says the Lord (Isaiah 55:8). Merit does not consist in doing or giving much, but in receiving, in loving much. It is said that "it is more blessed to give than to receive" (Acts 20:35), and that is true; but when Jesus wants to make His own the blessedness of giving, it would not be gracious to refuse. Let Him take and give what He chooses, perfection consists in doing His will; and the soul which gives itself totally to Him is called by Jesus "His mother, His sister," and His whole family (Matthew 12:50). And more than that: "If anyone love Me, he will keep My word (which means, he will do My will) and My Father will love him and We will come to him and make Our abode with him" (John 14:23)....How easy it is to give pleasure to Jesus, to enrapture His heart! All one has to do is love Him, not considering oneself, not examining one's faults too closely....My director, Jesus, does not teach me to count my acts, but to do everything for love, to refuse Him nothing, to be pleased when He gives me a chance to prove to Him that I love Him—but all this in peace, in abandonment, Jesus does everything, I nothing.

Letter to Céline, July 6, 1893

If a man loves You and acknowledges Your goodness,
he should find joy above all else
in the fulfillment in his own life
of Your will and of Your everlasting decree.
That should bring him so much contentment and happiness
that he is just as ready to be the least
as others are to be the greatest;
just as peaceful and contented in the lowest place
as he would be in the highest,
and just as ready to be despised and rejected
and have no fame or reputation,
as to be honored and important.

The Imitation of Christ, Book 3, XXII, 127

The Heart Is Opened by Love Alone

Listen to me, Yahweh, answer me,
for I am poor and needy.
Guard me, for I am faithful,
save your servant who relies on you....
Lord, you are kind and forgiving,
rich in faithful love for all who call upon you.
Yahweh, hear my prayer,
listen to the sound of my pleading....
But you, Lord, God of tenderness and mercy,
slow to anger, rich in faithful love and loyalty,
turn to me and pity me.
Give to your servant your strength,
to the child of your servant your saving help,
give me a sign of Your kindness.
My enemies will see to their shame
that you, Yahweh, help and console me.

Psalm 86:1–2,5–6,17–18

Later on my present state may appear as most imperfect, but nothing surprises me anymore, and I am not distressed when my helplessness is brought home to me; on the contrary, I make it my boast, and expect each day to reveal some imperfection which I had not seen before.

This enlightenment on my nothingness does me more good, in fact, than enlightenment on matters of faith. I remember that "charity covereth a multitude of sins" (Proverbs 10:12) and draw upon the riches opened up by Our Lord in the Gospels. I search the depths of His adorable words, and cry with David: "I have run in the way of Thy commandments when Thou didst enlarge my heart" (Psalm 118:32).

My heart is opened out by charity alone....O Jesus, ever since this heart of mine has been consumed by its gentle flame I have run in the way of Your new commandment with delight, and may I go on doing so until the day, when, in Your company of virgins, I will follow You throughout the boundless spaces of eternity, singing Your new canticle, the canticle of love.

The Story of a Soul, IX, 126

If only you had once seen the unfading crowns
of the saints in Heaven,
the great glory that fills with joy
those who once were thought of no account
in the eyes of the world,
not worthy even to live!
Then you certainly humble yourself to the ground,
and would strive to be the servant of all
rather than the master of one.
The Imitation of Christ, Book 3, XLVII, 159

At the Heart of the Church Is Love

There are many different gifts, but it is always the same Spirit;
there are many different ways of serving, but it is always the
same Lord....
Now Christ's body is yourselves, each of you with
a part to play in the whole....
Set your minds on the higher gifts.
And now I am going to put before you the best way of all.

1 Corinthians 12:4–5,27,31

I went on reading, and found relief in the following advice;
"Be zealous for the better gifts. And I show unto you a
yet more excellent way" (1 Corinthians 12:31). The Apostle
goes on to explain that the most perfect gifts are worth nothing
without love, and this more excellent way of going to God is
Charity.

At last I was at rest! As I thought about the Church's Mystical
Body I could not see myself in any of the members mentioned
by Saint Paul, or rather, I wanted to see myself in all of them.

Charity gave me the key to my vocation. I saw that if the
Church was a body made up of different members, the most
essential and important one of all would not be lacking; I saw
that the Church must have a heart, that this heart must be on
fire with love. I saw that it was love alone which moved her
other members, and that were this love to fail, apostles would
no longer spread the Gospel, and martyrs would refuse to shed
their blood. I saw that all vocations are summed up in love, and

that love is all in all, embracing every time and place because it is eternal.

In a transport of ecstatic joy I cried: "Jesus, my love, I have at last found my vocation; it is love. I have found my place in the Church's heart, the place You Yourself have given me, my God. Yes, there in the heart of Mother Church I will be Love; so shall I be all things, so shall my dreams come true."

I have used the expression "ecstatic joy," but this is not quite correct, for it is above all peace which is now my lot; the calm security of the sailor in sight of the beacon guiding him to port. Ah! Love, my radiant beacon light, I know the way to reach You now, and I have found the hidden secret of making all Your flames my own!

The Story of a Soul, XI, 156

May I love You more than myself,
and myself only because of You;
and in You let me love all those who truly love You.
The law of love that shines from You gives us this com-
mand.

The Imitation of Christ, Book 3, V, 102

He Loves Us Even to Folly

There is no room for self-delusion.
Any one of you who thinks he is wise by worldly standards
must learn to be a fool in order to be really wise.
For the wisdom of the world is folly to God....

but you belong to Christ and Christ belongs to God....
Here we are, fools for Christ's sake.

1 Corinthians 3:18–19,23; 4:10

We have only the brief instant of life that we can give to the good God...already He is preparing to say: "My turn now."...What a happiness to suffer for Him who loves us even to folly, and to pass for fools in the eyes of the world. One judges others by oneself, and as the world is stupid it naturally thinks that we are the stupid ones!...

But after all, we are not the first! The one crime charged against Jesus by Herod was that He was mad...and I agree with him!... Yes, it was folly to seek the poor little hearts of mortals to make them His thrones, He, the King of Glory, Who is throned above the Cherubim! He Whose presence is mightier than the Heavens can contain! Our Beloved was mad to come down to earth seeking sinners to make them His friends, His intimates, to make them like unto Himself, when He was perfectly happy with the two adorable Persons of the Trinity!... We shall never be able to commit the follies for Him that He has committed for us, nor do our actions deserve the name of folly, for they are in fact most reasonable acts, far below what our love would like to accomplish. So that it is the world which is stupid, not realizing what Jesus has done to save it. It is the world which is the all-devouring thing, seducing souls and leading them to "fountains without water" (Jeremiah 2:13).

Letter to Céline, August 19, 1894

When I think of these wonderful things
even spiritual comfort becomes distasteful to me,
because as long as I am not seeing my Lord openly
and in His glory,
I can find no value in anything I see or hear in this world.
O God, You know it is true that nothing can comfort me,
that no created thing can satisfy my longing,
but only You, my God, whom I yearn to gaze on for ever.
But that is impossible as long as I remain
in this mortal body;
so I must be prepared to exercise patience,
and with all my desiring, to submit myself to You.
The Imitation of Christ, Book 4, XI, 205

Love Pushed Even to Heroism

Then Job stood up, tore his robe and shaved his head.
Then, falling to the ground, he prostrated himself and said,
"Naked I came from my mother's womb,
naked I shall return again.
Yahweh gave, Yahweh has taken back.
Blessed be the name of Yahweh!"
In all this misfortune Job committed no sin,
and he did not reproach God.

Job 1:20–22

The Little Way

What then has Jesus done, so to detach our souls from every created thing? Ah! He has struck us a great blow, but a blow of love….God is admirable, but above all He is lovable, so let us love Him…let us love Him enough to suffer for Him whatever He chooses, even griefs of soul, aridities, anguish, seeming frigidities. Ah! that is indeed a great love, to love Jesus without feeling the sweetness of that love, there you have martyrdom….All right! Let us die martyrs!

Martyrdom unrealized by men, known to God alone, undiscoverable by the eye of any creature, martyrdom without honor, without triumph….There you have love pushed even to heroism. But one day a grateful God will cry out: "My turn now." Oh! what shall we see then? What is that life, to which there shall be no end?

Letter to Céline, July 14, 1889

When you feel little or no devotion in your heart,
then is the time to humble yourself;
but you must not be too dejected, nor unduly despondent,
for God often gives in one brief moment
what He has long been keeping from you,
and sometimes grants at the end of your prayer
the thing He has held back at first.
If grace were always given quickly
and could be had for the asking,
it would prove more than feeble mankind could endure.
That is why you have to wait for the grace of devotion
with a good hope and humble patience.

The Imitation of Christ, Book 4, XV, 212

The Proof of Love

But what were once my assets I now through Christ Jesus
count as losses. Yes, I will go further: because of the supreme
advantage of knowing Christ Jesus my Lord, I count
everything else as loss. For him I have accepted the loss of
all other things, and look on them all as filth
if only I can gain Christ and be given a place in him,
with the uprightness I have gained not from the Law,
but through faith in Christ, an uprightness from God,
based on faith, that I may come to know him
and the power of his resurrection,
and partake of his sufferings
by being molded to the pattern of his death,
striving towards the goal of resurrection from the dead.
Not that I have secured it already, not yet reached my goal,
but I am still pursuing it in the attempt to take hold of
the prize for which Christ Jesus took hold of me.

Philippians 3:7–12

To keep Jesus' word—that is the sole condition of our happiness, the proof of our love for Him. But what is this word?...
It seems to me that Jesus' word is Himself, Jesus, the Word (John
1:1), the Word of God!...He says so further on, in the same
Gospel of Saint John. Praying to His Father for His disciples, He
expresses Himself thus: "Sanctify them by Thy word, Thy word
is truth" (John 17:17). In another place Jesus tells us that He is
the Way and the Truth and the Life (John 14:6). We know then
what the Word is that we must keep. We do not, like Pilate, ask

Jesus "What is truth?" (John 18:38). We possess Truth, we keep Jesus in our hearts!...

Often we can say with the Spouse that our Beloved is a bundle of myrrh (Song of Songs 1:13), that He is for us a "betrothed in blood" (Exodus 4:25), but how sweet it will be one day to hear that most loving word proceed from Jesus' mouth: "And you are they who have continued with Me in my temptations: and I dispose to you, as my Father has disposed to Me, a kingdom!" (Luke 22:28–29).

The temptations of Jesus, what mystery is there! So He too has His temptations! He has indeed. And often He "treads the winepress alone. He seeks for those who may give Him aid and finds none" (Isaiah 63:3,5). Many serve Jesus when He consoles them, but few are willing to keep company with Jesus sleeping on the waves or suffering in the garden of agony! Who then will be willing to serve Jesus for Himself?

Letter to Céline, July 7, 1894

As long as I am detained in the prison of the body
I need two things,
and they are light and food.
Therefore you have given Your holy Body
to strengthen my weak mind and body,
and You have given Your word for a lamp to guide my feet.
Without these two things I cannot live as I ought,
for the word of God is the light of my soul,
and Your sacrament the bread that gives me life.
The Imitation of Christ, Book 4, XI, 206

Love, Even to Folly

But Yahweh is waiting to be gracious to you,
the Exalted One, to take pity on you,
for Yahweh is a God of fair judgment;
blessed are all who hope in him.
Yes, people of Zion living in Jerusalem,
you will weep no more.
He will be gracious to you when your cry for help rings out;
as soon as he hears it, he will answer you.

Isaiah 30:18–19

Oh, how lucky you are to have a heart that can love so…. Thank Jesus for having made you so precious a gift, and give Him your heart whole and entire. Creatures are too small to fill the immense void that Jesus has hollowed out in you, give them no place in your soul….

The good God will not catch you in His nets, for you are already wholly caught up in them….

Yes, it is surely true that our affection is not of this world, it is too strong for that, death itself could not break it….

Do not be worried at feeling no consolation in your communions; that is a trial that must be borne with love, do not waste any of the thorns that you meet every day; with one of them you can save a soul!…

Ah! if you knew how the good God is insulted! Your soul is so well made to console Him… love Him, even to folly, for all those who do not love Him!

Letter to Marie Guérin, July 14, 1889

If you desire the grace of devotion,
you must seek it unceasingly,
ask for it earnestly,
and wait for it with patience and faith.
When it comes you must receive it thankfully,
preserve it humbly,
use it thoughtfully;
and leave to God the time and way in which
He will visit you from Heaven,
waiting till He comes.

> *The Imitation of Christ, Book 4, XV, 212*

Your Heart Is Made to Love Jesus

For God created human beings to be immortal,
he made them as an image of his own nature;
Death came into the world only through the Devil's envy,
as those who belong to him find to their cost....
But the souls of the upright are in the hands of God,
and no torment can touch them....
Those who trust in him will understand the truth,
those who are faithful will live with him in love;
for grace and mercy await his holy ones,
and he intervenes on behalf of his chosen.

> *Wisdom 2:23–24; 3:1,9*

The devil...realizes, treacherous creature that he is, that he cannot get a soul to sin if that soul wants to belong wholly to Jesus, so he only tries to make it think it is in sin. It is already much for him to have put confusion into that soul, but his rage demands something more; he wants to deprive Jesus of a loved tabernacle; since he cannot enter that sanctuary himself, he wants at least to have it remain empty and without master....

When the devil has succeeded in keeping a soul away from Holy Communion, he has gained all...and Jesus weeps!...Do you realize that Jesus is there in the tabernacle expressly for you, for you alone? He burns with the desire to come into your heart.... Don't listen to the demon, laugh at him, and go without fear to receive the Jesus of peace and love!...

No, it is not possible that a heart "that finds no rest save in the sight of the tabernacle" should offend Jesus enough to be unfit to receive Him. What offends Jesus, what wounds His heart, is want of trust!...

Your heart is made to love Jesus, to love Him passionately.... We have only the brief moments of this life to love Jesus, the devil is well aware of it, so he tries to consume it in futile occupations....Receive Communion often, very often....There you have the sole remedy if you want to be cured.

Letter to Marie Guérin, May 30, 1889

For the Wicked Spirit himself,
as it says in the Book of Job (1:6–7),
comes among the sons of God, so that he can upset them
with his practiced villainy,

and make them fearful or perplexed;
he hopes in this way to weaken their desire
or attack their faith and destroy it....
But you must not pay any attention
to his tricks and suggestions....
People are often hindered by being too anxious
to feel devotion,
and by worrying about their confession.
Follow the advice of the wise and lay aside worry and
doubt,
because they are a hindrance to the grace of God
and destroy the spirit of devotion.

The Imitation of Christ, Book 4, X, 202

Our God, Our Heart's Guest

Do you not realize that you are a temple of God
with the Spirit of God living in you?
If anybody should destroy the temple of God,
God will destroy that person,
because God's temple is holy;
and you are that temple.

1 Corinthians 3:16–17

"How shall we sing the songs of Sion in a strange land? For long we have hung up our harps on the willows by the river" (Psalm 137:4,2), for we cannot play on them!...Our God, our heart's Guest knows it well, so He comes within us in the intent of finding a dwelling place, an empty tent, in the midst of the world's battlefield. He asks no more than that, and He is Himself the divine Musician who is responsible for the harmony. Ah! if we could hear that unutterable harmony, if one single vibration could reach our ears!...

"We know not what we should pray for as we ought, but the Spirit Himself asks for us with unspeakable groanings" (Romans 8:26). So all we have to do is deliver up our soul, abandon it to our great God. What does it matter then if it is without any exteriorly brilliant gifts, since, within, the King of Kings stands brilliant in all His glory!

How great must a soul be to be able to contain a God! Yet the soul of a day-old child is for Him a paradise of delights; what then will our souls be, that have fought and suffered to ravish the Heart of their Beloved?

Letter to Céline, July 7, 1894

It is a pure heart that I seek, and there I take My rest.
Prepare Me a large upper room, furnished,
and I will eat the paschal meal
at your house with My disciples.
If you want Me to come to you and stay with you,
you must rid yourself of the leaven which remains over;
you must clean the house of your heart.
The Imitation of Christ, Book 4, XII, 208

Tell Him That You Love Him

Always be joyful, then, in the Lord; I repeat, be joyful.
Let your good sense be obvious to everybody.
The Lord is near.
Never worry about anything;
but tell God all your desires of every kind
in prayer and petition shot through with gratitude,
and the peace of God which is beyond our understanding
will guard your hearts and your thoughts in Christ Jesus.

Philippians 4:4–7

I am begging Jesus to let the sun of His grace shine upon your soul. Ah! don't be afraid to tell Him that you love Him, even though you have no feeling of love, that is the way to force Jesus to come to your help, to carry you like a little child too weak to walk.

It is a great trial to see everything black, but this is a matter not wholly within your control, do what you can. Detach your heart from the cares of the world and especially from creatures, then be sure that Jesus will do the rest. He cannot let you fall into the slough that you fear. Stop worrying, in Heaven you won't see everything black, you'll see everything white.

Letter to Sister Marthe of Jesus, ?1894

It's because we think of the past and the future that we become discouraged and fall into despair.

Said to Mother Agnes of Jesus, August 19, 1897

I am more pleased to see patience and humility
when things are difficult,
than a state of devotion and spiritual joy
when things go well.
Whatever the trouble, put it out of your heart
as best you can;
even if it does touch you, do not let it depress you,
or keep you concerned for too long.
If you cannot bear it joyfully, bear it patiently, at least…
I am still living, says the Lord,
and I am ready to help you and comfort you
more than you have ever known,
if you trust Me and call on Me devoutly
The Imitation of Christ, Book 3, LVII, 178

Love Him More Than Self

Even were I to walk in a ravine as dark as death
I should fear no danger, for you are at my side.
Psalm 23:4

Then Jesus took me by the hand and brought me into a sub-terranean way, where it is neither hot nor cold, where the sun does not shine, and rain and wind do not come; a tunnel where I see nothing but a brightness half-veiled, the glow from the downcast eyes in the Face of my Spouse.

My Spouse says nothing to me, nor do I say anything to Him either, save that I love Him more than myself and in the depth of my heart I feel that this is true, for I am more His than my own!...

I do not see that we are advancing towards the mountain that is our goal, because our journey is under the earth; yet I have a feeling that we are approaching it, without knowing why.

The road I follow is one of no consolation for me, yet it brings me all consolations because it is Jesus who has chosen it, and I desire to console Him only.

Letter to Sister Agnes of Jesus, September 1890

> *Call to mind that old saying—*
> *eye looks on unsatisfied,*
> *ear listens ill-content*
> *Make it your aim to detach your heart*
> *from the love of things which can be seen,*
> *and to transfer all your affections*
> *to things which cannot be seen.*
> *The Imitation of Christ, Book 1, I, 34*

Love Lives in Us

I have called you by your name, you are mine.
Should you pass through the waters, I shall be with you;
or through rivers, they will not swallow you up.
Should you walk through fire, you will not suffer
and the flame will not burn you.

Tranquil Trust

For I am Yahweh, your God,
the Holy One of Israel, your Savior.

Isaiah 43:1b–3a

How marvelously our spouse calls us! Think! We did not dare even to look at ourselves, so utterly dull and unadorned we felt: and Jesus calls us. He wants to gaze on us at leisure, but He is not alone, with Him come the other two Persons of the Blessed Trinity to take possession of our soul….Jesus promised it long ago when He was on the point of ascending to His Father and our Father. He said with tenderness unutterable: "If anyone love Me, he will keep My word and My Father will love him and We will come to him and will make our abode with him" (John 14:23).

Letter to Céline, July 7, 1894

But who am I, Lord, to presume to approach You?
The very heavens cannot contain You, and yet You say,
"Come to Me, all of you"?
What does it mean, this affection and kindness,
this loving invitation?
How dare I come, when I know
there is no goodness in me to give a right to come?
How can I bring You into my house,
when I have so often offended Your kindly eyes?
The angels and archangels feel awe before You,
the saints and the upright fear—
and yet You say, "Come to Me, all of you"?

The Little Way

If anyone said this but You, Lord,
who would believe it was true?
If anyone called us but You, Lord,
who would dare to draw near?
The Imitation of Christ, Book 4, I, 186

4

Persistence in Prayer
As a Simple Raising
of the Heart to God

In your prayers do not babble....
your Father knows what you need before you ask him.
Matthew 6:7–8

Prayer, for me, is simply a raising of the heart,
a simple glance towards Heaven,
an expression of love and gratitude.
The Story of a Soul, X, 135

Make time to attend to your inner life
and frequently think over the benefits God has given you.
The Imitation of Christ, Book 1, XX, 56

Introduction

So often, to many people, the words "pray" and "prayer" con-
jure up an image of a book being opened so that prayers
can be recited from it to an unseen and, hopefully, listening
God. But the Christian, following the new law of love taught by
Jesus, is part of a tradition which is unique among the diversity
of world religions in emphasizing the personal, involved, and
loving Fatherhood of God.

If in everyday life a child were invited by its parent to sit with
him or her and talk in a personal exchange and the child were
to respond by going to the bookshelves and reading from a book
to the parent, it would be felt that the child had misunderstood.
The parent looks to the child for its own words, its own reac-
tions and feelings. The passage from the book may be relevant,
even, but of itself it is not personal—unless, of course, it was
brought into the conversation to illustrate or underline some
aspect of the exchange.

Thérèse, like so many of us, was brought up to rely heavily
on set vocal prayers and devotional books. Nevertheless, her
pursuit of a direct, personal relationship and exchange with
God is shown by her answer when young to her teacher's query
as to what she did with her free time. Thérèse replied, "I very
often hide in a little corner of my room which I can easily close
off…and there I reflect…I think of the good Lord…well, I *think*."
Jesus had, of course, told His disciples, "When you pray, go to
your private room, shut yourself in and so pray to your Father"
(Matthew 6:6). Later, she heard a nun explain how she talked
to God "with the heart"; this revelation encouraged Thérèse in

her developing understanding of personal prayer as an action of love, a free and liberated giving and receiving.

In her mature years, Thérèse retained and deepened her conception of personal prayer as a simple turning to God in which the individual is able to respond to the approach which God makes to each of His children, in which each is offered his or her own unique relationship and exchange with Him. Each affair of love is special and different from all others.

In Thérèse's case, her prayer life was often arid and dry and not, as one might surmise from her writings and sayings, full of consolation. This only made her the more determined to persist in her simple raising of the heart to God, her many glances toward Heaven.

Thérèse also greatly loved and valued—and was assisted by—community prayer, where set forms and words are necessary so as to create unity of intention and action. Each way of prayer, personal and community, supports and sustains the other. Together they make concrete the universal love and praise of God. Indeed, the daily prayers of the Church are used by many to help provide a regular rhythm and pattern of prayer and praise—a launch pad from which the heart is lifted off to its own spontaneous, free expression to God. As Saint Augustine said, "Love, then do what you will."

Prayer Unites the Soul With God

In your prayers do not babble as the gentiles do,
for they think that by using many words
they will make themselves heard.
Do not be like them;
your Father knows what you need before you ask him.

Matthew 6:7–8

The power of prayer is certainly wonderful. One might liken it to a queen who always has free access to the king and can obtain everything she asks.

It is not necessary to read from a book beautiful prayers composed for our particular need before we can be heard. If this were the case, I should certainly have to be pitied.

The daily recitation of the Divine Office is a great joy to me in spite of my unworthiness, but apart from this I have not the courage to make myself search for wonderful prayers in books; there are so many of them, and it gives me a headache. In any case, each one seems more beautiful than the one before. As I can't say all of them, and do not know which to choose, I just act like a child who can't read; I tell God, quite simply, all that I want to say, and He always understands.

Prayer, for me, is simply a raising of the heart, a simple glance towards Heaven, an expression of love and gratitude in the midst of trial as well as in times of joy; in a word, it is something noble and supernatural expanding my soul, and uniting it to God.

Whenever my soul is so dry that I am incapable of a single good thought, I always say an Our Father or a Hail Mary very slowly, and these prayers alone cheer me up and nourish my soul with divine food.

The Story of a Soul, X, 135

So whatever desirable scheme presents itself to you,
you must be governed by humility and the fear of God
as you work towards it;
above all, you must commit it entirely to Me,
abandoning your own will, and saying:
Lord, You know what is best.
May Your will decide what shall be done.
Give what You will, how much You will,
and when You will.
Do what You know is best for me, do what pleases You
and brings Your Name most honor.

The Imitation of Christ, Book 3, X, 116

Meditate on the Gospel

For the reasoning of mortals is inadequate,
our attitudes of mind unstable;
for a perishable body presses down the soul,
and this tent of clay weighs down the mind
with its many cares.
It is hard enough for us to work out what is on earth,
laborious to know what lies within our reach;
who, then, can discover what is in the heavens?

Persistence in Prayer

And who could ever have known your will,
had you not given Wisdom
and sent your holy Spirit from above?
Thus have the paths of those on earth been straightened
and people have been taught what pleases you,
and have been saved, by Wisdom.

Wisdom 9:14–18

Whenever I open a book, no matter how beautiful or touching, my heart dries up and I can understand nothing of what I read; or if I do understand, my mind will go no further, and I cannot meditate. I am rescued from this helpless state by the Scriptures and the Imitation, finding in them a hidden manna, pure and substantial; but during meditation I am sustained above all else by the Gospels. They supply my poor soul's every need, and they are always yielding up to me new lights and mysterious hidden meanings. I know from experience that "the Kingdom of God is within us" (Luke 17:21), and that Jesus has no need of books or doctors to instruct our soul; He, the Doctor of Doctors, teaches us without the sound of words. I have never heard Him speak, and yet I know He is within my soul. Every moment He is guiding and inspiring me, and just at the moment I need them, "lights" till then unseen are granted me. Most often it is not at prayer that they come but while I go about my daily duties.

The Story of a Soul, VIII, 105

In the Holy Scriptures we must look for truth, not eloquence.
All Scripture must be read in the spirit in which it is writ-
ten, and in the Scriptures we look for what will help us,
and not for subtle points.
When we read the Scriptures, we are often hindered
by our own curiosity,
because we want to know and discuss
where we ought simply to read on.
If you want to drink in spiritual benefit,
read in humility, simplicity, and faith,
and at no point desire to be known for your learning.
The Imitation of Christ, Book 1, V, 39

Prayer Uplifts the World

"Be still and acknowledge that I am God,
supreme over nations, supreme over the world."
Psalm 46:10

We will run, indeed, all of us, for souls on fire with love can-not remain inactive. Like Mary, they may sit at the feet of Jesus, listening while His gentle words inflame their love, giving Him nothing, so it seems, and yet really giving Him more than a Martha who is anxious about "many things" (Luke 10:41). Not that Jesus condemns the work she is doing, only the fuss she makes about it; after all, His own Mother humbly performed those very same tasks when she used to prepare meals for the Holy Family.

Persistence in Prayer

It is a lesson which all the saints have understood, particularly those who have spread the light of the Faith throughout the world. Saint Paul, Saint Augustine, Saint Thomas Aquinas, Saint John of the Cross, Saint Teresa of Avila and so many other friends of God; surely it was in prayer that they acquired that wonderful knowledge which captivates even the greatest of minds.

"Give me a fulcrum," said Archimedes, "and with a lever I will move the world." He was asking the impossible, and yet this is just what the saints have been given. Their fulcrum is none other than Mighty God Himself, their lever, prayer, the prayer which enkindles the fire of love. It is with this lever that they have uplifted the world, and with this lever those who are still fighting in the world will go on raising it until the end of time.

The Story of a Soul, X, 148

In all that happens you must not stop short
at external appearances,
or look at sights and sounds with human sense;
on every occasion you must go at once with Moses
into the Tabernacle,
and ask the Lord's advice.
Then you will often hear God's answer,
and come back wiser to deal with present and future.
The Imitation of Christ, Book 3, XXXVIII, 148

A Simple Prayer for Others

Delicate is the fragrance of your perfume,
your name is an oil poured out....
Draw me in Your footsteps, let us run.
The king has brought me into his rooms;
you will be our joy and gladness.
We shall praise your love more than wine;
how right it is to love you.

Song of Songs 1:3a,4

Though I have only these two brothers and my sisters the novices, my days are not long enough to detail all their needs, and I would probably forget something really important. Complicated methods are not for simple souls like me; so Our Lord Himself has inspired me with a very simple way of fulfilling my obligations.

One day after Communion He taught me the meaning of the following words in the Canticle of Canticles: "Draw me...we will run after Thee to the odor of Thy ointments" (Song of Songs 1).

It is therefore unnecessary, my Jesus, to say "draw those I love in drawing me." It is quite enough to say simply "Draw me." For once a soul has been captivated by the odor of Your ointments, she cannot run alone; by the very fact of being drawn to You herself, she draws all the souls she loves after her. Just as a mighty river carries with it all it meets into the ocean's depths, so, my Jesus, a soul which plunges into the boundless ocean of Your love bears all her treasures with her. You know what

my treasures are; they are the souls You made one with mine,
treasures which You Yourself have given me.

The Story of a Soul, X, 145

> *I am the foundation of all the saints...*
> *I know the merits of each one—*
> *I went before them with the blessings of My sweetness;*
> *I knew My beloved from the first before all ages.*
> *I singled them out from the world—*
> *they did not first choose Me.*
> *I called them by My grace,*
> *I drew them by My mercy....*
> *I embrace them all with a love that cannot be told.*
> *Imitation of Christ, Book 3, LVIII, 180*

Love Draws Us to Pray for Others

Wisdom speaks her own praises....
"I came forth from the mouth of the Most High,
and I covered the earth like mist."...
From eternity, in the beginning, he created me,
and for eternity I shall remain.
In the holy tent I ministered before him
and thus became established in Zion.
In the beloved city he has given me rest,
and in Jerusalem I wield my authority.

I have taken root in a privileged people,
in the Lord's property, in his inheritance....
Like cinnamon and acanthus, I have yielded a perfume,
like choice myrrh, have breathed out a scent.

Ecclesiasticus 24:1a,3,9–12,15

B ut I have not told you yet all that this passage from the Canticle of Canticles means to me: "Draw me...we will run."

"No man," says Our Lord, "can come to Me, except the Father, who has sent Me, draw him" (John 6:44); and later He teaches us that we have only to knock and it will be opened to us; to seek and we shall find; to hold out our hands humbly, and they will be filled; adding that "if you ask the Father anything in My name, He will give it to you" (John 16:23).

I am sure that is why the Holy Spirit, long before Jesus was born, inspired this prophetic prayer, "Draw me, we will run." In asking to be drawn, we are seeking to be closely united to the captivating object of our love.

If fire and iron were endowed with reason, and the iron were to say "Draw me," surely this would prove that it wanted to be so identified with the fire as to share its very substance. This is just what I ask. I want Jesus so to draw me into the flames of His love, so as to make me one with Himself, that He may live and act in me. I feel that the more the fire of love inflames my heart, the more I shall say "Draw me," and the more swiftly those who are around me will run "in the sweet odor of the Beloved."

The Story of a Soul, X, 147

I am the foundation of all the saints…
They are all one, bound together by love.
Their thoughts and their wills are one,
and mutual love unites them; and what is nobler still,
they love Me more than themselves, and their own merits.
They are rapt outside themselves,
raised beyond the love of self;
they pass altogether into love for Me,
and there they rest in joy.
Nothing can turn them away or cast them down from there,
for they are filled with the eternal truth,
and burn with the flame of inextinguishable love.
The Imitation of Christ, Book 3, LVIII, 180

Prayer Works Miracles

We have then, brothers, complete confidence through the
blood of Jesus in entering the sanctuary.…
Do not lose your fearlessness now, then,
since the reward is so great.
You will need perseverance if you are to do God's will
and gain what he has promised.…
We are not the sort of people who draw back, and are lost by it;
we are the sort who keep faith until our souls are saved.
Hebrews 10:19,35–36,39

We must not grow weary of praying. Confidence works miracles and Jesus told Blessed Margaret Mary: "One just soul has so much power over My Heart that it can obtain from it pardon for a thousand criminals." No one knows whether he himself is just or sinful, but Jesus gives us the grace to feel in the very depth of our heart that we would rather die than offend Him. And in any event it is not our merits but those of our Spouse, which are ours, that we offer to our Father who is in Heaven, in order that our brother, a son of the Blessed Virgin, should come back vanquished to throw himself beneath the cloak of the most merciful of mothers.

Letter to Céline, July 8, 1891

My brother,
do not throw away that confidence you have
of attaining spiritual things—
there is still time and opportunity.
But why put off making your resolve?
Stand up and begin this moment; say to yourself:
Now is the time for action,
now is the time for battle,
now is the right time to mend my ways.
The Imitation of Christ, Book 1, XXII, 61

Only God Supplies All Needs

There is a season for everything,
a time for every occupation under heaven....
A time for searching,
a time for losing;
a time for keeping,
a time for discarding....
What do people gain from the efforts they make?
I contemplate the task that God gives humanity to labor at.
All that he does is apt for its time;
but although he has given us an awareness
of the passage of time,
we can grasp neither the beginning nor the end
of what God does.

Ecclesiastes 3:1,6,9–11

Speaking of the visits by her sister Céline (named Sister Geneviève on her entry to Carmel) when Céline was taking care of her ill father, Saint Thérèse said:

When Sister Geneviève used to come to visit me, I wasn't able to say all I wanted to say in a half-hour. Then, during the week, whenever I had a thought or else was sorry for having forgotten to tell her something, I would ask God to let her know and understand what I was thinking about, and in the next visit she'd speak to me exactly about the thing I had asked God to let her know.

At the beginning, when she was really suffering and I was unable to console her, I would leave the visit with a heavy heart, but I soon understood it wasn't I who could console anyone; and then I was no longer troubled when she left very sad. I begged God to supply for my weakness, and I felt He answered me. I would see this in the following visit. Since that time, whenever I involuntarily caused anyone any trouble, I would beg God to repair it, and then I no longer tormented myself with the matter.

Said to Mother Agnes of Jesus, July 13, 1897

I also bring You all the holy desires of those who love You,
the needs of parents, friends, brothers, sisters,
of all I hold dear,
and of all who for love of You have done some kindness
to myself or others,
and who have asked me to say prayers and Masses
for themselves and all they love,
whether they are still in the body
or whether they have gone from this world.
May they all know the help of Your grace.

The Imitation of Christ, Book 4, IX, 201

Jesus Supplies, Moment to Moment

Surely Yahweh's mercies are not over,
his deeds of faithful love not exhausted;
every morning they are renewed;
great is his faithfulness!
"Yahweh is all I have," I say to myself,
"and so I put all my hope in him."
Yahweh is good to those who trust him,
to all who search for him.
It is good to wait in silence
for Yahweh to save.
Lamentations 3:22–26

I must tell you about my retreat for profession. Far from experiencing any consolation, complete aridity—desolation, almost—was my lot. Jesus was asleep in my little boat as usual. How rarely souls let Him sleep peacefully within them. Their agitation and all their requests have so tired out the Good Master that He is only too glad to enjoy the rest I offer Him. I do not suppose He will wake up until my eternal retreat, but instead of making me sad, it makes me very happy.

Such an attitude of mind proves that I am far from being a saint. I should not rejoice in my aridity, but rather consider it as the result of lack of fervor and fidelity, while the fact that I often fall asleep during meditation, or while making my thanksgiving should appall me. Well, I am not appalled; I bear in mind that little children are just as pleasing to their parents asleep as awake; that doctors put their patients to sleep while they perform operations, and that after all, "the Lord knoweth our frame. He remembereth that we are but dust" (Psalm 52:14).

My retreat for profession, as I was saying, was spent in great aridity, as were those that followed, but without my being aware of it, the way to please God and practice virtue was being made clear to me. I have often noticed that Jesus will not give me a store of provisions; He nourishes me with food that is entirely new from moment to moment, and I find it in my soul without knowing how it got there. In all simplicity, I believe that Jesus Himself is, in a mysterious way, at work in the depths of my soul inspiring me with whatever He wants me to do at that moment.

The Story of a Soul, VIII, 93

> *I have never found anyone so religious and devout*
> *that he did not sometimes feel grace withdrawn*
> *and fervor lessened.*
> *There has never been a saint so caught up to heaven*
> *and illumined*
> *that he was not tempted either before or after....*
> *Temptation is often the sign of comfort to come,*
> *for it is to those who have been tried in temptation*
> *that the comfort of heaven is promised....*
> *The devil does not go to sleep,*
> *and the old nature is not yet dead.*
> *Therefore you must not cease to prepare yourself for battle,*
> *for an enemy who never rests surrounds you*
> *to right and to left.*

The Imitation of Christ, Book 2, IX, 86

Throw Straws on the Fire of Love

I am filled with love when Yahweh listens
to the sound of my prayer,
when he bends down to hear me, as I call....
Deliver me, Yahweh, I beg You.
Yahweh is merciful and upright,
our God is tenderness.
Yahweh looks after the simple,
when I was brought low he gave me strength.
Psalm 116:1–2,4–6

Saint Teresa [of Avila] says we must feed the fire of love. When we are in darkness, in dryness, there is no wood within our reach, but surely we are obliged at least to throw little bits of straw on the fire. Jesus is quite powerful enough to keep the fire going by Himself, yet He is glad when we add a little fuel, it is a delicate attention which gives Him pleasure, and then He throws a great deal of wood on the fire; we do not see it but we feel the strength of Love's heat.

I have tried it: when I feel nothing, when I am incapable of praying or practicing virtue, then is the moment to look for small occasions, nothings that give Jesus more pleasure than the empire of the world, more even than martyrdom generously suffered. For example, a smile, a friendly word, when I would much prefer to say nothing at all or look bored, etc....

Do you understand? It is not to make my crown, to gain merits, but to give pleasure to Jesus....When I find no occasions, at least I want to keep telling Him that I love Him, it's not difficult and it keeps the fire going; even if that fire of love were to seem wholly out, I should throw something on it and then Jesus could relight it....Perhaps you will think that I always act like this. Oh, no! I am not always faithful, but I am never discouraged, I abandon myself in Jesus' arms.

Letter to Céline, July 18, 1893

It is I that called you;
I commanded this to be done;
I will supply your deficiencies....
When I give you the grace of devotion,
thank your God for it,
not because you deserved it,
but because I have taken pity on you.
If on the other hand you find yourself
unable to produce any emotion,
give yourself to prayer;
call out and beat on the door.
  The Imitation of Christ, Book 4, XII, 208

Jesus' Peace Never Leaves

The bonds of death were all round me,
the snares of Sheol held me fast;
distress and anguish held me in their grip,
I called on the name of Yahweh.
Deliver me, Yahweh, I beg You....

Persistence in Prayer

My trust does not fail even when I say,
"I am completely wretched."
In my terror I said,
"No human being can be relied on."
What return can I make to Yahweh
for his generosity to me?
I shall take the cup of salvation
and call on the name of Yahweh.

Psalm 116:3–4,10–13

He knows of course that if He let me have the bare shadow of happiness I should cling to it with all the energy, all the strength of my heart: this shadow He refuses me!...He would rather leave me in darkness than give me a false light that would not be Himself.

Since I can find no created thing to content me, I will to give all to Jesus, I will not give to a creature even an atom of my love; may Jesus grant me always to realize that He alone is perfect happiness, even when He seems to be absent!...

Today more than yesterday, if that be possible, I have been without any consolation. I thank Jesus, since He sees that that is good for my soul; perhaps, if He gave me consolations, I should rest in their sweetness, but He wants all to be for Him! Good! Then all shall be for Him, all! Even when I feel nothing that can be offered to Him, I shall (as tonight) give Him that nothing!... If Jesus does not give me consolation, He gives me a peace so great that it does me more good!

Letter to Sister Agnes of Jesus, January 7 or 8, 1889

The voice of the Lord:
It is Mine to comfort the mourner with new hope,
and it is those that know their own weakness
that I raise to My divinity.
The disciple:
Lord, blessings on what You have said…
Remember me, O my God, and guide me by a straight path
to Your kingdom.
Amen.

The Imitation of Christ, Book 4, LVII, 179

Merely a Sigh, a Prayer of the Heart

May Yahweh add to your numbers,
yours and your children too!
May you be blessed by Yahweh,
who made heaven and earth.

Psalm 115:14–15

R ecently a thought has struck me….One day I was pondering over what I could do to save souls; a phrase from the Gospel showed me a clear light; Jesus said to his disciples, pointing to the fields of ripe corn: "Lift up your eyes and see the countries. For they are white already to the harvest" (John 4:35), and a little later, "The harvest indeed is great, but the laborers are few. Pray ye therefore the Lord of the harvest that He send forth laborers" (Matthew 9:37–38).

How mysterious it is! Is not Jesus all-powerful? Do not creatures belong to Him who made them? Why then does Jesus say: "Pray ye the Lord of the Harvest that he send forth laborers"?

Why?...Surely because Jesus has so incomprehensible a love for us, that He wants us to have a share with Him in the salvation of souls. He wants to do nothing without us. The Creator of the universe waits for the prayer of a poor little soul to save other souls redeemed like itself at the price of all His blood.

Our vocation, yours and mine, is not to go harvesting in the fields of ripe corn; Jesus does not say to us; "Lower your eyes, look at the fields, and go and reap them"; our mission is still loftier. Here are Jesus' words: "Lift up your eyes and see...." See how in My Heaven there are places empty; it is for you to fill them....Each one of you is My Moses praying on the mountain; ask Me for laborers and I shall send them, I await only a prayer, a sigh from your heart.

Letter to Céline, August 15, 1892

O Lord my God...
To offer thanks and praise along with me
I invite and exhort by my prayers and longings
all heavenly spirits and all Your faithful people.
Let all people praise You, all tribes and tongues,
and let them with jubilation and burning love
praise Your holy Name,
as sweet as honey on the tongue.
The Imitation of Christ, Book 4, XVII, 215

Offer Everything, in Happy Praise

If we say, "We have no sin," we are deceiving ourselves,
and truth has no place in us;
if we acknowledge our sins, he is trustworthy and upright,
so that he will forgive our sins
and will cleanse us from all evil....
Our fearlessness towards him consists in this,
that if we ask anything in accordance with his will,
he hears us.
And if we know that he listens to whatever we ask him,
we know that we already possess
whatever we have asked of him.

1 John 1:8–9; 5:14–15

In reply to her sister Pauline, Mother Agnes of Jesus, who was confiding her thoughts of sorrow and discouragement after having committed a fault, Saint Thérèse said:

You don't act like me. When I commit a fault that makes me sad, I know very well that this sadness is a consequence of my infidelity, but do you believe I remain there? Oh! no, I'm not so foolish! I hasten to say to God: My God, I know I have merited this feeling of sadness, but let me offer it up to You just the same as a trial that You sent me through love. I'm sorry for my sin, but I'm happy to have this suffering to offer to You.

Said July 2, 1897

To all three of her sisters, Saint Thérèse said:

D on't believe that when I'm in heaven I'll let ripe plums fall into your mouths. This isn't what I had, nor what I desired. You will perhaps have great trials, but I'll send you lights which will make you appreciate and love them. You will be obliged to say like me: "Lord, You fill us with joy with all the things You do for us" (Psalm 91:5).

Said July 13, 1897

Holy Father,
this was Your command, Your will;
what You decreed has come to pass.
When I am asked to endure suffering and trouble
in this world for love of You,
however frequent it may be and whatever its cause,
I count it as a favor shown by You to a friend.
It was good for me to blush with confusion,
so that I should look to You for comfort
rather than men.

The Imitation of Christ, Book 3, L, 165

5

*Daily Practice
of the Little Way
of Love*

So always treat others as you would like them to treat you.
Matthew 7:12

A love that does not prove itself in action is not enough.
The Story of a Soul, IX, 121

*You have read all this and know it—
you will be blessed if you put it into practice.*
The Imitation of Christ, Book 3, LVI, 177

Introduction

There is an apparent paradox in Saint Thérèse's teachings. She was convinced that God "has no need of our works—He has need of our love." Equally, she was convinced that "a love that does not prove itself in action is not enough."

It would seem that God does not need our activity of itself, for He has all power and can in a moment achieve what we struggle, and fail, to do over so much time. But equally, knowing that we of ourselves will fail, He nevertheless looks to each of us for that goodwill which is necessary if we are to be open to His action. We are little and unable. We are weak and incapable. But, seeing us show our goodwill by our attempts to reflect and mirror His love, He will then say, "My turn now—I will do what you want."

Thérèse quoted the saying of Saint John of the Cross that the smallest act of pure love is of greater value than all other works put together. Her insight taught her that, while some singular souls are given the means to perform great works, most of us are little, too little to perform great actions. But because of that very fact, we can all the more trust God to accept our incapable efforts (and our actual failures) and grant us still greater favors commensurate with our needs. The more we are little and weak, the more we will be given favors.

God is drawn to our weakness. He accepts the smallest, the least, act of real love on our part. Then, with a "love which reaches even unto folly," He will act for us, in a creative collaboration between the Father and the child, between Creator and creature.

But we must remain little and keep trying—and with Saint John of the Cross say, "Now I occupy myself and all my energy in His service." Then, the paradox provides a miracle.

Love Must Act

The whole group of believers was united, heart and soul;
no one claimed private ownership of any possessions,
as everything they owned was held in common.

Acts 4:32

A love which does not prove itself in action is not enough, nor is our natural readiness to please a friend; that is not charity, for sinners are ready to do the same. Jesus also teaches me to "give to everyone that asketh thee; and of him that taketh away thy goods, ask them not again" (Luke 6:30). It is much harder to give to all who ask than to offer our services spontaneously; nor is it so hard to comply with a friendly request, but if we happen to be asked in a tactless way, we are at once up in arms, unless we are rooted in perfect charity. We find countless excuses, and only after we have made it quite clear to the Sister that she is lacking in courtesy do we condescend to grant her request as a favor, or we do something for her which probably takes a twentieth of the time wasted in making excuses and insisting on our imaginary rights.

If it is hard to give to everyone who asks, it is harder still to let them take things away from us without asking for them back again. I say it is hard; I should rather say it seems hard, for "the yoke of the Lord is sweet and His burden light" (Matthew 11:30), and as soon as we accept it, we realize that. The fact that Jesus does not want me to ask for anything back should seem to me natural enough, since nothing I have really belongs to me. I ought to rejoice when I have to put my vow of Poverty into practice.

The Story of a Soul, IX, 121

There is no one free from weakness,
no one without a load to carry,
no one who is self-sufficient,
no one who can dispense with others' help,
and so it is our duty to support each other,
to comfort each other,
to help, guide and advise each other.
The Imitation of Christ, Book 1, XVI, 50

The Truly Poor Are Happy

For wherever your treasure is, that is where
your heart will be too.

Luke 12:34

I used to think I was detached from everything, but now...I realize how imperfect I am.

If, for example, I find my brushes all over the place when starting to paint, or if a ruler or penknife has disappeared, I have to take strong hold of myself to resist demanding them back with asperity. As I really need them, there is no harm in asking, and I am not going against what Jesus asks if I do so in all humility; on the contrary, I am only acting like the poor, who hold out their hands for alms and are not surprised if they are refused because nobody owes them anything. What peace floods a soul when it soars above natural feelings! The joy of the truly poor in spirit is beyond all compare; when they ask disinterestedly for something they need, and not only is it refused, but what they already have is taken away, they follow Our Lord's advice: "If any man take away thy coat, let go thy cloak also unto him" (Matthew 5:40). To surrender our cloaks, so it seems to me, is to surrender our last rights, to consider ourselves as everyone's servant and slave.

When we have given away our coat we can walk more easily, we can run, so Jesus adds: "and whosoever will force thee one mile, go with him another two" (Matthew 5:41). It is not even enough for me to give to all who ask; I must go beyond their desires, and show myself very honored, and only too glad to offer my services. If some thing which I normally use is taken away, I should appear happy to be rid of it.

I can't always carry out these words of the Gospel to the letter; there are bound to be times when I have to refuse my Sisters something. But when we are deeply rooted in charity, we can always find a way to refuse so charmingly that our refusal gives more pleasure than the gift would have done.

The Story of a Soul, IX, 122

The man who has true and perfect love
does not seek his own advantage in anything,
but desires only that God may be glorified in all things.
He feels no envy towards anyone,
because he has no desire for any pleasure that is not
shared;
nor does he want any joy that springs from self,
because he desires to find his happiness above all good gifts
in God.

The Imitation of Christ, Book 1, XV, 49

God Loves Others Through Us

You should all agree among yourselves and be sympathetic;
love the brothers, have compassion and be self-effacing.
Never repay one wrong with another,
or one abusive word with another;
instead, repay with a blessing.

1 Peter 3:8–9

Under the Old Law, when God told His people that they must love their neighbor as themselves, it was before He had come upon earth Himself; knowing how much man loved himself, it was the best He could ask. But when Jesus gives His Apostles a New Commandment (John 13:34), His own Commandment (John 15:12), He asks them to love one another, not only as they love themselves, but as He Himself loves them, and will love them even unto the consummation of the world!

Yet I know, my Jesus, that You never command the impossible; You know better than I do how frail and imperfect I am; You know perfectly well that I can never hope to love my Sisters as You love them unless You Yourself love them in me.

It is only because You are willing to do this that You have given us a New Commandment, and I love it because it is my assurance of Your desire to love in me all those whom You command me to love.

I know that whenever I am charitable, it is Jesus alone who is acting through me, and that the more closely I unite myself to Him, the more I will be able to love all my Sisters.

Should the devil draw my attention to the faults of any one of them when I am seeking to increase this love in my heart, I call to mind at once her virtues and her good intentions. I tell myself that though I may have seen her fall once, there are probably a great many other occasions on which she has won victories which, in her humility, she has kept to herself. What may appear to me to be a fault may even be an act of virtue because of her intention; and as I have experienced this for myself, I have little difficulty in persuading myself that this is indeed the case.

The Story of a Soul, IX, 119

Real wisdom and perfection lie in having no high opinion of oneself,
but in always thinking highly of others.
Even if you see another man openly doing wrong,
or committing some fault,

you should not consider yourself better than he is,
for you do not know how long you can avoid a fall.
We are all of us weak,
but you should consider yourself the weakest of all.
The Imitation of Christ, Book 1, II, 35

Giving Love for Jesus

And you, little child,
you shall be called Prophet of the Most High,
for you will go before the Lord
to prepare a way for him,
to give his people knowledge of salvation
through the forgiveness of their sins,
because of the faithful love of our God
in which the rising Sun has come from on high to visit us,
to give light to those who live
in darkness and the shadow dark as death,
and to guide our feet into the way of peace.
Luke 1:76–79

Only Jesus is: everything else is not....Let us love Him then to the point of folly, let us save souls for Him....For our mission is to forget ourselves, to annihilate ourselves...we are so small a matter...yet Jesus wills that the salvation of souls should depend on our sacrifices, our love. He is a beggar begging us for souls....Let us understand the look on His face! So few can understand it. Jesus does us the marvelous favor of instructing us Himself, showing us a hidden light....Life will be short, eternity has no end. Let us make of our life a continual sacrifice, a martyrdom of love to console Jesus. He wants only a look, a sigh from us, but a look and a sigh that are for Him alone!...Let every instant of our life be for Him alone. Let creatures touch us only in passing....

There is but one sole thing to do during the night of this life, that single night which will come but once, and that is to love, to love Jesus with all the strength of our heart, and to save souls for Him that He may be loved....Oh! to make men love Jesus!

Letter to Céline, October 15, 1889

You must love all people for the sake of Jesus,
but you must love Jesus for Himself;
and Jesus Christ is the only person who may be loved
beyond all others,
for He alone is good and faithful, beyond all other friends.
For Jesus' sake, and in Jesus, you must value enemies
as well as friends,
and you must pray to Him for all of them,
so that all may learn to know and love Him.

The Imitation of Christ, Book 2, VIII, 83

Do Everything to Give Pleasure to Jesus

Let us love, then, because he first loved us.
Anyone who says "I love God" and hates his brother is a liar,
since no one who fails to love the brother whom he can see
can love God whom he has not seen.

1 John 4:19–20

Often a single word, a friendly smile, is enough to give a depressed or lonely soul fresh life.

Nevertheless, I do not always want to practice charity merely to bring consolation. I would soon be discouraged if that were so, for something said with the best of intentions may be taken completely the wrong way; so in order not to waste time and trouble, I try to do everything to give pleasure to Our Lord, and to follow out this Gospel precept: "When thou makest a supper, call not thy friends nor thy brethren, lest perhaps they also invite thee again and a recompense be made to thee. But when thou makest a feast, call the poor, the maimed, the blind and the lame, and thou shalt be blessed because they have naught to make thee recompense" (Luke 14:12–14). "And thy Father, who seeth in secret, will repay thee" (Matthew 6:4).

A spiritual feast of gentle, joyful love is all I can set before my Sisters; I do not know of any other, and want to follow the example of Saint Paul, rejoicing with all who rejoice. I know he wept with those who weep, and my feasts are not always without their share of tears, but I always try to turn them into smiles, for "the Lord loveth the cheerful giver" (2 Corinthians 9:7).

The Story of a Soul, X, 139

Give up self,
surrender yourself
and you will know great peace in your heart.
Give your all for the One who is All;
expect nothing,
want nothing back;
leave yourself with Me wholly and without regrets,
and you will possess Me.

The Imitation of Christ, Book 3, XXXVII, 147

Unselfish Love Is Joyful

If anyone gives so much as a cup of cold water
to one of these little ones because he is a disciple,
then in truth I tell you, he will most certainly
not go without his reward.

Matthew 10:42

In the time of the law of fear, before the coming of Our Lord, the prophet Isaiah, speaking in the name of the King of Heaven, could say: "Can a mother forget her child? And if she should forget, yet will not I forget thee" (Isaiah 49:15). What ecstasy in that promise! Ah! and we who live under the law of love, how can we fail to put to profit the loving advances our Spouse makes to us? How can we fear One "who lets himself be held by a hair of our neck?" (Song of Songs 4:9). So we must learn to hold Him prisoner, this God who makes Himself a mendicant for our love. In telling us that a hair can work so great a marvel,

126

He is showing that the smallest actions done for love are the actions which win His heart. Ah! if we had to do great things, how much to be pitied we should be!...But how fortunate we are, since Jesus lets Himself be held by the smallest!...You have no lack of small sacrifices, is not your life made up of them?...It is so sweet a thing to aid Jesus by our slight sacrifice, to aid Him to save the souls He has redeemed at the price of His blood, souls which await only our help not to fall into the abyss.

It seems to me that if our sacrifices are hairs to hold Jesus prisoner, so are our joys; to make them so, it is enough that we are not concentrated in a selfish happiness but that we offer our Spouse the small joys He sows in life's path to win our souls and raise them to Him.

Letter to Léonie, July 12, 1896

Who can come to the well of sweetness
without carrying away even a little sweetness with him?
Who can stand near the blazing fire
without absorbing a little warmth?
The Imitation of Christ Book 4, IV, 194

Love Others As Jesus Loves Them

Since by your obedience to the truth
you have purified yourselves
so that you can experience the genuine love of brothers,
love each other intensely from the heart;

for your new birth was not from any perishable seed
but from imperishable seed,
the living and enduring Word of God.

1 Peter 1:22–23

I have received countless graces this year, but the one I value most is the one of understanding the precept of charity in all its fullness. I had never fully understood before what Our Lord meant when He said: "The second commandment is like the first. Thou shalt love thy neighbor as thyself" (Matthew 22:39). I had concentrated on loving God, but in loving Him I came to realize the meaning of those other words of His: "Not everyone that saith to Me, Lord, Lord, shall enter into the Kingdom of Heaven, but he that doth the will of My Father" (Matthew 7:21).

Now, Jesus made known His will to me at the Last Supper, when He gave His Apostles His New Commandment: "Love one another as I have loved you" (John 13:34). I set to work to discover how Jesus had loved them. I found that He had not loved them for their natural qualities, for they were ignorant and taken up with earthly things, yet He called them His friends and His brothers (John 15:15; 20:17) and wanted to have them with Him in His Father's Kingdom; He was ready to die on the cross to make this possible, saying: "Greater love than this no man hath, that a man lay down his life for his friends" (John 15:13).

Meditating on these divine words, I saw only too well how very imperfect was my love for my Sisters; I did not really love them as Jesus loves them.

I see now that true charity consists in bearing with the faults of those about us, never being surprised at their weaknesses, but edified at the least sign of virtue. I see above all that charity must not remain hidden in the bottom of our hearts, for "no man lighteth a candle and putteth it in a hidden place, nor under a bushel; but upon a candlestick, that they who come in may see the light" (Luke 11:33). It seems to me that this candle is the symbol of charity; it must shine out not only to cheer those we love best but all those who are of the household.

The Story of a Soul, IX, 118

Turn your eyes on yourself,
and beware of judging the actions of others.
In judging others a man expends efforts to no purpose,
he is often mistaken and easily sins.
The Imitation of Christ, Book 1, XIV, 48

Love and Do Not Judge

Be compassionate just as your Father is compassionate.
Do not judge, and you will not be judged;
do not condemn, and you will not be condemned;
forgive, and you will be forgiven.
Give, and there will be gifts for you:
a full measure, pressed down, shaken together,
and overflowing,
will be poured into your lap;
because the standard you use
will be the standard used for you.

Luke 6:36–38

It was one day during recreation. The Portress came to ask one of us to help her in some particular duty. I was as eager as a child to do this work, and as it happened, I was chosen. Though I began to put away my needlework at once, I did so sufficiently slowly to give my neighbor a chance of folding hers first, because I knew she would be glad to take my place.

The Portress noticed that I was taking my time, and said laughingly: "I did not think you would add this pearl to your crown: you were much too slow." The whole community was left with the impression that I had acted according to nature.

I cannot tell you what I gained from this incident and how tolerant it made me. Praise is no longer an occasion of vanity. I have only to say to myself: "If my little acts of virtue can be mistaken for imperfections, imperfections can just as easily be mistaken for virtue: and I say with Saint Paul: "To me it is a very small thing to be judged by you, or by man's day. But neither do I judge myself. He that judgeth me is the Lord" (1 Corinthians 4:3–4).

I too am judged by the Lord; I am judged by Jesus. I will never think uncharitably of anyone so that He may judge me leniently, or rather, not at all, for He has said: "Judge not, and ye shall not be judged" (Luke 6:37).

I turned to the Gospels again, where Our Lord explains clearly His New Commandment: "You have heard that it hath been said, Thou shalt love thy neighbor and hate thy enemy: but I say unto you, love your enemies and pray for them that persecute you" (Matthew 5:43–44).

Of course we have no enemies in Carmel, but we do have to contend with our natural feelings; one Sister attracts us, while we would go out of our way to avoid meeting another. Jesus tells me that it is this very Sister I must love; I must pray for her even though she shows no sign of loving me. "If you love them that love you, what thanks are to you? For sinners also love those that love them" (Luke 6:32).

The Story of a Soul, X, 120

Love feels no burden, and counts up no toil;
it aspires to do more than its strength allows;
it does not plead impossibility
but considers that it may do and can do all things.
So it finds strength for anything.
The Imitation of Christ, Book 3, V, 102

Offer the Merits of Others to Jesus

God was in Christ reconciling the world to himself,
not holding anyone's faults against them,
but entrusting to us the message of reconciliation.
So we are ambassadors for Christ.
2 Corinthians 5:19–20a

There was at that time a certain nun who managed to irritate me in everything she did. The devil had a part in it, for it was certainly he who made me see all her bad points. Not wishing to give way to natural antipathy, I reminded myself that sentiments of charity were not enough; they must find expression, and I set myself to treat her as if I loved her best of all.

I prayed for her whenever we met, and offered all her virtues and merits to God. I was sure that Jesus would be delighted at this, for artists always like to have their work praised, and it pleases the Divine Artist of souls when, not stopping at the exterior, we penetrate the inner sanctuary where He dwells, to admire its beauty.

I prayed earnestly for this Sister who had caused me so much struggle, but this was not enough for me. I tried to do everything I possibly could for her, and when tempted to answer her sharply I hastened to give her a friendly smile, and talk about something else; for, as it says in the *Imitation,* "It is better to leave everyone to their own way of thinking than begin an argument."

Sometimes, when the devil made a particularly violent attack, if I could slip away without letting her suspect my inward struggle, I would run away from the battle like a deserter; and what was the result?

She said to me one day, her face radiant: "What do you find so attractive in me? Whenever we meet you give me such a gracious smile." What attracted me? It was Jesus hidden in the depths of her soul, Jesus who makes attractive even what is most bitter.

I have just mentioned my last resort in escaping defeat in the battle of life…to act like a deserter. It is not very honorable, but it has always proved successful, and I often used it during my novitiate.

The Story of a Soul, IX, 124

Put true and trustworthy words in my mouth,
and see that my tongue is never crafty.
I must avoid doing at all costs
what I do not want others to do to me.
The Imitation of Christ, Book 3, XLV, 156

A Strange Courage

Now this Lord is the Spirit,
and where the Spirit of the Lord is,
there is freedom.

2 Corinthians 3:17

Here is an example which will probably make you smile. You had been ill for some days with bronchitis, and I was rather anxious. One morning I came softly to your infirmary to put away the keys of the communion grille, for I was sacristan. I was secretly rejoicing at this chance to see you, but one of the Sisters was afraid I was going to wake you up, and in her zeal tried to relieve me of the keys.

I told her very politely that I was just as anxious as she was to make no noise, but that it was my duty to replace them. I know now that it would have been better if I had simply handed them to her, but I did not think so at the time. I tried to push my way in, in spite of her opposition.

Then it happened...the noise we were making awakened you, and everything was blamed on me! The Sister made quite a speech, the burden of which was: "It was Sister Thérèse of the Child Jesus who made all the noise."

I simply longed to defend myself, but happily I had a bright idea. I knew I would certainly lose my peace of mind if I tried to justify myself; I knew too that I was not virtuous enough to remain silent in the face of this accusation. There was only one way out—I must run away. No sooner thought than done; I fled!...but my heart was beating so violently that I could not go very far, and I sat down on the stairs to enjoy quietly the fruits of victory.

A strange kind of bravery, but it was better than exposing myself to certain defeat!

The Story of a Soul, IX, 125

A man is easily upset by censure
when he does not keep his thoughts centered within him
and his eyes fixed on God;
but the man who trusts in Me
and does not attempt to stand by his own judgment
will be free from the fear of men.
The Imitation of Christ, Book 3, XLVI, 157

Serving Jesus in Others

Be servants to one another in love,
since the whole of the Law is summarized
in the one commandment:
"You must love your neighbor as yourself."
Galatians 5:13b–14

I remember one act of charity, inspired by God, when I was still a novice. It did not seem much, but our Heavenly Father "who seeth in secret" has rewarded me already in this life, without my having to wait for the next. It was before Sister Saint Peter became a complete invalid. At ten to six every evening, someone had to go out from meditation to take her along to the Refectory. It cost me a lot to offer my services, because I knew how difficult she was to please, almost impossible, but it was a wonderful chance, and I did not want to miss it. I remembered the words of Our Lord, "As long as you did it to one of these My brethren, you did it to Me" (Matthew 25:40). So very humbly I offered to help her, and after a lot of trouble, she was prevailed upon to accept me...and then a real ceremony began....

I had to go behind her, and support her by her girdle, and I used to do this as gently as I possibly could; but if by some mischance she chanced to stumble, she thought I was not holding her properly; she was going to fall over: "My goodness! you are going much too fast. I shall hurt myself." I try to go more slowly. "Why don't you keep up with me? I don't feel your hand. You are letting me go. I shall fall over! How right I was when I said you were much too young to look after me!"

At last we arrived at the Refectory without any more mishaps. Then there was more trouble! She had to be maneuvered into her place very skillfully so as not to be hurt in any way, her sleeves must be rolled back, again just so, then I could go.

It was not long before I noticed that she could not cut her bread very easily, so I used to do that too before finally leaving her....I always gave her, so she said, my "very best smile."

I was carrying out my usual task one winter evening; it was cold and dark. Suddenly, far away, from some distant orchestra, there came the sound of music. I seemed to see a richly furnished room, all bright with lights, and resplendent, where young ladies, beautifully dressed, exchanged the countless courtesies of society life. My eyes turned back to the poor invalid I was helping. In place of the music, plaintive groans from time to time; in place of the resplendent room, nothing but the cloister walls, austere, scarcely visible in the flickering light. I would not exchange the ten minutes spent upon my act of charity for a thousand years of such worldly delights.

The Story of a Soul, X, 139

If you relished these things,
and they really had a meaning in your heart,
would you dare utter a single complaint?
The Imitation of Christ, Book 3, XLVII, 159

Love in Adversity

For the fig tree is not to blossom,
nor will the vines bear fruit,
the olive crop will disappoint,
and the fields will yield no food;
the sheep will vanish from the folds;
no cattle in the stalls.
But I shall rejoice in Yahweh,
I shall exult in God my Savior.
Yahweh my Lord is my strength,
he will make my feet as light as a doe's,
and set my steps on the height.
Habakkuk 3:17–19

For a long time I had to kneel during meditation near a Sister who could not stop fidgeting; if it was not with her Rosary, it was with goodness knows what else. Maybe no one else noticed it; I have a very sensitive ear. But you have no idea how much it annoyed me. I wanted to turn round and glare at the culprit to make her be quiet, but deep in my heart I felt that the best thing to do was to put up with it patiently for the love of God first of all, and also not to hurt her feelings. So I kept quiet, bathed in perspiration often enough, while my prayer was nothing more than the prayer of suffering! In the end I tried to find some way of bearing it peacefully and joyfully, at least in my inmost heart; then I even tried to like this wretched little noise.

It was impossible not to hear it, so I turned my whole attention to listening really closely to it as if it were a magnificent concert, and spent the rest of the time offering it to Jesus. It was certainly not the prayer of quiet!

The Story of a Soul, X, 141

While you live in the flesh,
the burden of the flesh will prove a sorrow to you,
for it will not let you devote yourself
to spiritual thoughts and contemplation of God
without interruption.
At such times it is best for you to turn to
lowlier outward activities,
and refresh your soul in good works,
confidently waiting for Me to come and visit you
from on high;
and bear your exile and the dryness of your soul
with patience,
until I come to you again
and you are freed from all your anxieties.
For I will make you forget your unhappiness
and grant you peace in your heart.

The Imitation of Christ, Book 3, LI, 167

Washed by Love

I shall pour clean water over you, and you will be cleansed;
I shall cleanse you of all your filth and of all your foul idols.
I shall give you a new heart, and put a new spirit in you;
I shall remove the heart of stone from your bodies
and give you a heart of flesh instead.

Ezekiel 36:25–26

Another time, washing handkerchiefs in the laundry opposite a Sister who kept on splashing me with dirty water, I was tempted to step back and wipe my face to show her that I would be obliged if she would be more careful. But why be foolish enough to refuse treasures offered so generously? I took care to hide my exasperation.

I tried hard to enjoy being splashed with dirty water, and by the end of half an hour, I had acquired a real taste for this novel form of aspersion. How fortunate to find this spot where such treasures were being given away! I would come back as often as I could.

So you see, Mother, what a very little soul I am! I can only offer very little things to God. These little sacrifices bring great peace of soul, but I often let the chances of making them slip by. However, it does not discourage me. I put up with having a little less peace, and try to be more careful the next time.

The Story of a Soul, X, 142

The Little Way

The voice of the Lord:
You must resolutely aim at being inwardly free
and your own master,
in every place and in every outward deed and occupation.
See that things are under you, not over you.
Where your actions are concerned, be master and ruler,
not slave or servant.
Be a free man, a true Hebrew,
transferred to the status and freedom of the sons of God,
who stand above temporal things
and spy out the eternal.

The Imitation of Christ, Book 3, XXXVIII, 147

Sources and Bibliography

The selected texts given in this book are from:

The New Jerusalem Bible, London: Darton, Longman & Todd, Ltd. and Doubleday, a division of Bantam Doubleday Dell Publishing Group, Inc., 1985.

The Story of a Soul, The Autobiography of St. Thérèse of Lisieux, translated by Michael Day, Cong. Orat., from the 1898 edition by Mother Agnes of Jesus, Anthony Clarke Books, 1990. Chapter and page numbers are included in the references given with these texts.

St. Thérèse of Lisieux, Her Last Conversations, translated by John Clarke O.C.D., Washington D.C.: ICS Publications, 1977. References commencing "Said to" relate to this book.

Collected Letters of Saint Thérèse of Lisieux, translated by F. J. Sheed, London: Sheed and Ward, 1989. References commencing "Letter to" relate to this book.

The Imitation of Christ by Thomas à Kempis, translated by Betty I. Knott, London: Fount Paperbacks, HarperCollins, 1990. Book, chapter, and page numbers are included in the references given with these texts.

Available translations of the autobiography of St Thérèse, other than that by Michael Day referred to on the previous page, include:

The Autobiography of Saint Thérèse *of Lisieux—The Story of a Soul*, translated by John Beevers from the 1898 edition by Mother Agnes of Jesus, New York: Image Books, Doubleday, 1989.

Thérèse *of Lisieux—Autobiography of a Saint*, translated by Ronald Knox from the 1956 publication of the original manuscript as written by Saint Thérèse, London: Fount Paperbacks, Harper Collins, 1991.

Story of a Soul—The Autobiography of Saint Thérèse *of Lisieux*, translated by John Clarke O.C.D, from the 1972 publication of the original manuscript as written by Saint Thérèse; Washington D.C.: ICS Publications, 1976.

Sources and Bibliography

Other helpful books on the Saint are:

Thérèse of Lisieux: A Life of Love, Jean Chalon, Liguori, MO: Liguori Publications, 1997.

St. Thérèse of Lisieux by Those Who Knew Her (Testimonies from the process of beatification), edited and translated by Christopher O'Mahoney, Dublin: Veritas Publications, 1975.

Holy Daring, The Fearless Trust of Saint Thérèse of Lisieux, John Udris; Herefordshire, Gracewing, 1997.

The Little Way: The Spirituality of Thérèse of Lisieux, Bernard Bro, O.P., translated by A. Neame, London: Darton, Longman and Todd, 1997.

The Spiritual Journey of St. Thérèse of Lisieux, Guy Gaucher, O.C.D., Homebush, Australia: St. Paul Publications, 1989.

The Passion of Thérèse of Lisieux, Guy Gaucher, O.C.D., Homebush, Australia: St. Paul Publications, 1989.

The Spiritual Genius of Saint Thérèse of Lisieux, Jean Guitton, Liguori, MO: Liguori/Triumph, 1997.

Complete Spiritual Doctrine of St. Thérèse of Lisieux, Francois Jamart, O.C.D., New York: St. Paul Publications, 1961.

Thérèse of Lisieux: A Biography, Patricia O'Connor, Huntington, IN: Our Sunday Visitor, 1997.

My Vocation Is Love: Thérèse of Lisieux, Jean Lafrance, Homebush, Australia: St. Paul Publications, 1961.

Ways of Imperfection, Simon Tugwell, O.P., Springfield, IL: Templegate Publishers, 1985. (See Chapter 18.)

The Photo Album of St. Thérèse of Lisieux, translated by Peter-Thomas Rohrbach, Westminster, MD: Christian Classics, 1990.

CPSIA information can be obtained
at www.ICGtesting.com
Printed in the USA
LVOW04s0259260716

497798LV00027B/315/P